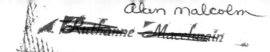

SIG...
CHRIST'S

as Son of Man

By

CARL ARMERDING

MOODY PRESS

CHICAGO

First Moody Press Edition, 1965

Revised Edition © 1971 by
THE MOODY BIBLE INSTITUTE
OF CHICAGO

ISBN: 0-8024-0545-2

CONTENTS

3

PREFACE

MOST OF THE MATERIAL in this book appeared first in a series of articles published in the *Moody Monthly* magazine. It deals with events occurring in what is quite commonly known as "the seventieth week of Daniel." Our Lord's reference to the setting up of "the abomination of desolation," which will take place in the middle of that week, confirms this (cf. Mt 24:15 and Dan 12:11). After this event takes place "there shall be a thousand two hundred and ninety days" (Dan 12:11), or three and a half years. This is the latter half of the seventieth week of years, and it will be a time of unparalleled tribulation (see Mt 24:9, 21, 25, ASV). That week will begin with the confirmation of an important covenant (Dan 9:27), and will conclude with the gathering together of "his elect from the four winds, from one end of heaven to the other" (Mt 24:31; Is 43:5-6).

Nothing is said here about the resurrection of the dead in Christ, or of the saints going to meet Him in the air. Since these are two outstanding features of the rapture of the church described in 1 Thessalonians 4:13-18 and 1 Corinthians 15:51-54, we conclude that this gathering does not refer to the rapture but to the gathering of Israel whom Jehovah calls His elect (Is 45:4). May this study serve to stir our hearts to pray, "Even so come, Lord Jesus."

CARL ARMERDING

5

1

THE TIME OF THE END

MATTHEW 24:1-14

THE GOSPEL according to Matthew includes three important discourses or sermons by the Lord Jesus Christ. The first is the well-known Sermon on the Mount in chapters 5-7. The second, which occupies all of chapter 13, consists of a series of parables known as the parables of the kingdom. The third, in chapters 24 and 25, is generally referred to as the Olivet discourse because of the locality in which it was delivered.

Each of these discourses refers in one way or another to the earthly kingdom of Christ. The Sermon on the Mount is frequently referred to as the constitution of that kingdom because in it we get the principles of its government. Here is found the Lawgiver who is greater than Moses, saying again and again, "But I say unto you," as He lays down the rules that are to govern His subjects.

The parables of the kingdom present the various phases of that kingdom from its inception to the day when the King shall send forth His angels to gather out of His kingdom all things that offend. The Olivet discourse is concerned particularly with this last phase of the kingdom, and with the coming of the King to inaugurate His earthly reign.

The Olivet discourse covers a shorter period of time than either of the other discourses. In it are an intensity and a rapidity of movement which are not in the others. Because it will be for the most part a time of unparalleled anguish and sorrow, it is aptly called the tribulation, and the latter part, the great tribulation.

This is not the first mention of the tribulation in the Bible. In their descriptions of "the day of the Lord," Isaiah, Jeremiah, Joel and others give details so exactly like those given here that there can be no question that they refer to the same time. (Cf., for example, Is 13:6-13 with Mt 24:21-30.) This is not to say that there have not been partial fulfillments of those Old Testament prophecies in time past, but the Olivet discourse is about a final fulfillment.

Daniel is the only one of the prophets who is referred to by name in Matthew 24 and 25. This is appropriate in view of the fact that when the disciples inquired about "the time of the end" they were talking about something which is mentioned in the prophecy of Daniel more than in any other book of the Old Testament. (There is a vast difference between "the time of the end" and "the end of time." The disciples were not inquiring about the end of time but about the end of an age in which they, as Jews, were particularly interested.)

In His discourse on the parables of the kingdom, the Lord refers to this three times. In the Authorized Version it is called "the end of the world," but a footnote in the American Standard Version gives it more correctly as "the consummation of the age." The Lord interpreted the parable of the tares (Mt 13:36-43) as referring to a time of harvest when He will send forth His angels to gather out of His kingdom all things that offend. If this refers to "the end of the world," as is generally understood, there would be no need for gathering out those things which offend. This is manifestly a purging, but with no thought of destroying the world in the process. Those gathered out—the wicked—will be cast into a furnace of fire (Mt 13:42), but there is no hint here that the world and its works will be burned up at that time.

On the other hand, it is clear that this removal of the wicked from among the just does not refer to the removal of the church at the coming of the Lord. He will not use angels to accomplish that. "The Lord *himself* shall descend from heaven" to claim His own at that time. The removal of the wicked, moreover, is the exact opposite of that which will take place at the rapture. Then, too, there is not even a hint of the resurrection of "the dead in Christ" —an outstanding feature of the rapture—in the

Olivet discourse. Indeed, there is no reference whatsoever to resurrection in this portion of Scripture.

In Isaiah 13:9, it says "the day of the LORD cometh,
cruel both with wrath and fierce anger, to lay the land
desolate: and he shall destroy the sinners thereof out
of it." It is by angelic forces that He will accomplish
this, according to Matthew 13:41. These same forces
are similarly engaged later in this same chapter (v.
49), but this action "concerns neither Israel nor the
Church, as is plain by the interpretation which our
Lord Himself gives: it is the mercy to the Gentiles,
after the purpose of God as to the Church is complete.
. . . This is at the completion of the age, and while
coincident with the final harvesting of the wheatfield,
is a different thing from it. To the present time it
cannot apply . . . for *we* are not in the completion of
the age, which is, as our Lord explains, the time of
harvest."[1]

"The consummation of the age" has no reference
to the age in which we live. It is the broken-off end
of Daniel's seventy weeks, "the time of the end" to
which he refers so often in his prophecy (Dan 8:17,
19; 9:26; 11:6, 27, 35, 40; 12:4, 9, 13). It will be
"a time of trouble, such as never was since there was
a nation even to that same time" (Dan 12:1). Comparing this statement with the Lord's words in Matthew 24:21, both refer to the same time. And the
fact that the Lord adds "no, nor ever shall be" shows
that there will never be another such time.

The question raised by the disciples in Matthew 24:3 came as the result of the Lord's prediction concerning the temple: "There shall not be left here one stone upon another that shall not be thrown down" (Mt 24:2). But it is sometimes overlooked that He had just said that the nation Israel should not see Him henceforth until they should say, "Blessed is he that cometh in the name of the Lord" (Mt 23:39).

It is to that coming that the disciples refer when they ask, "What is the sign of Thy coming and completion of the age?" (Mt 24:3, Darby trans.). To make that question refer to the Lord's coming as promised in John 14:3 is to confuse things that differ. The church, although promised, had not yet been formed as such. It was not until the Holy Spirit came at Pentecost and baptized believers into one body that the New Testament church came into being as "the body of Christ." That being so, the church could not have had any part in the first sixty-nine weeks of Daniel. Neither will it have any part in the seventieth week.

It was not the coming of the Lord for His church about which the disciples were concerned at this time. As a matter of fact, just before His ascension they were still talking about the restoration of the kingdom to Israel (Ac 1:6). And what they had just heard from the lips of the Lord would only tend to deepen their concern for their people, their land, and their temple.

In keeping with this, note that when the Lord answers their question, He begins with that to which they, as Israelites, would be especially exposed. Many would come to them in His name saying, "I am Christ" (or, "I am Messiah"), and deceive many (Mt 24:4-5). One can hardly conceive of a true Christian being deceived by anyone making such a claim. But it can readily be understood how a Jew, waiting for the Messiah, might be deceived by a false Christ. Comparing this verse with the parallel passages in Mark 13:6 and Luke 21:8, it is evident how bold such false Christs may become, even to the point of claiming deity by saying, "I am." The word *Christ* is not in the original in either of those passages, a fact that is indicated in most Bibles by the use of italics.

In issuing this warning the Lord was not addressing His disciples as individuals only "but as representatives of others also who should succeed them, and that right down to the time of the end, when the greatest false Christ will appear that the world has ever seen, and when death will be the penalty threatened for resisting his pretensions."[2] Of this one, the "many antichrists" (1 John 2:18) of apostolic times were but the forerunners. The "spirit of antichrist" was even then in the world (1 John 4:3).

But the Lord now goes on to speak of that which

will affect the world as a whole. "Ye shall hear of wars and rumors of wars," said He. This not only fits modern times but it has been true again and again since the Lord uttered those words. Nevertheless, He told His own not to be troubled by that, for "the end is not yet." In spite of that plain statement, some people still insist that "wars and rumors of wars" are a sure sign that we are in "the time of the end."

Now it may be thought that Matthew 24:7 is merely an amplification of the preceding statement. But the increasing racial antagonism of today may well cause wonder as to whether this rising of nation against nation may not have some reference to that. Likewise, the expression "kingdom against kingdom" might well apply to the clash of political ideologies that trouble the world at this very moment. And the famines, pestilences and earthquakes here spoken of may be sounding out their sad preludes even now. These may be the physical counterparts of those social, political and economic convulsions and upheavals among the nations of the world.

But commenting on these, the Lord says, "All these are the beginning of sorrows," or "travail pains," "as if nature were pressing on to a birth of a new and better time, and could not rest content or quiet with present evil."[3]

From that which is worldwide and universal, the Lord now turns to that which has to do primarily

with His ancient people—of whom His disciples are
representatives. Matthew 24:9 (Darby trans.) states
that "then shall they deliver you up to tribulation."
Nothing is known of being in the life-span of the
disciples themselves which might be considered a
real fulfillment of this passage.

The Lord is referring here to an event which will
affect all Israel—something about which Moses
warned Israel in his day. "When thou art in tribulation [or, in thy tribulation], and all these things are
come upon thee, even *in the latter days,* if thou turn
to the LORD thy God, and shalt be obedient unto his
voice; (For the LORD thy God is a merciful God;)
he will not forsake thee, neither destroy thee, nor forget the covenant of thy fathers which he sware unto
them" (Deu 4:30-31).

The expression "the latter days" plainly indicates
that Moses was speaking as a prophet of that which
was to come upon the nation centuries later. And
here the Prophet like unto Moses speaks of the be-
ginnings of that same tribulation. Apparently it
will begin with the delivering up of Israel not by the
Lord Himself as in the days of the judges (Judg
2:14, et al) but by others.

How that is to be accomplished is not told here,
but passages in the Old Testament may shed light on
this. Daniel 9:26-27 says a prince shall come who
will confirm a covenant with many—that is, with
the mass of the Jewish people—for one week. That

"one week" is the last of the seventy weeks of Daniel.

Isaiah 28:14-22 tells about a covenant which they make with death and hell. It is not to be supposed that they would knowingly make a covenant with death and hell, yet these are the divine characterizations of those with whom they do covenant, and in whom they place their confidence. Little will they realize that they will be delivering themselves to tribulation when they sign that covenant. At the same time they will be delivering up their godly brethren, "the remnant."

Undoubtedly the remnant will oppose such a covenant: they will not accept the Antichrist, neither will they favor his unholy alliance with the Roman prince. They will be awaiting Another, the true Messiah (Is 25:9). And for His name's sake they will be hated of all; not simply because they are Jews but because of their loyalty to Him whom the world will not receive. And since this hatred will come from "all nations," it will be universal.

Such a thing could hardly take place while the church is on earth. In spite of the fact that there are some anti-Semites within the ranks of the professing church, the true church is still the Jew's best friend today. No true Christian could ever hate the Jew because of the Messianic hope, or because of his loyalty to the Messiah. And until it can be shown that the Jew is being universally hated for the sake of Messiah's name, it cannot be maintained that the time referred to in Matthew 24:9 has arrived.

Removal of the church will, in fact, make possible the revelation of that wicked one "whom the Lord shall consume with the spirit of his mouth, and shall destroy with the brightness of his coming." Then the pious Jew will not only be hated of all the Gentiles for Messiah's name's sake but he will be hated and betrayed by his apostate brethren also. Isaiah 66:5 says, "Hear the word of the LORD, ye that tremble at his word; your brethren that hated you, that cast you out for my name's sake, said, Let the LORD be glorified: but he shall appear to your joy, and they shall be ashamed."

At the same time many false prophets shall arise and shall deceive many. Their coming, like that of the wicked one, will be "after the working of Satan with all power and signs and lying wonders, and with all deceivableness of unrighteousness in them that perish; because they received not the love of the truth, that they might be saved" (2 Th 2:9-10). It will be a time of lawlessness such as even this present age cannot match. And because of the prevalent lawlessness, the love of many shall wax cold. The majority will be marked by an utter lack of natural love and affection. And that accounts, in part at least, for the treason and hatred mentioned in Matthew 24:10.

It is in direct connection with such a time that the

Lord says, "But he that shall endure unto the end, the same shall be saved." It will be recalled that the Lord used this same expression when He commissioned the twelve to preach the gospel of the kingdom (Mt 10:5-22). Evidently that is the same gospel which is referred to here. Those who preach it will be subjected to much bitter persecution. Their endurance in and through it all will be a proof of the reality of their faith.

In a time like this when the Lord will plead with all flesh "by fire and by His sword," He will send "those that escape" unto the nations which have not heard His fame, neither have seen His glory, and the escaped remnant shall proclaim His glory among the Gentiles (Is 66:15-19). The universal authority of the Lord Jesus will be proclaimed in all the world, and that "testimony will reach all nations before the coming of that judgment which will put an end to the age" (Darby).

Such are the ways of the God of all grace, and thus does He illumine that which presents one of the darkest pages in all of the Scripture. "O the depth of the riches both of the wisdom and knowledge of God! How unsearchable are his judgments, and his ways past finding out!" (Ro 11:33).

2

THE SIGN OF THE TIME OF THE END

MATTHEW 24:14-22

IT MUST BE REMEMBERED that in the Olivet discourse the Lord Jesus Christ was answering three questions asked Him by His disciples (Mt 24:3). He began by warning them against a special form of deception which will be attempted by the enemy in "the time of the end." He also told them that "the time of the end" would be preceded by wars and rumors of wars, as well as other international disturbances, such as racial and political antagonisms and economic disorders. But He said these are only the beginning of sorrows or travail pains.

He also spoke of events which will have particular reference to His ancient people, the Jews, who will then be delivered up to tribulation. This will be brought about by some official act, such as that referred to in Daniel 9:27. And since that has not yet taken place, obviously He was speaking to the disciples as representatives of a generation yet to come.

In that generation there will be a group who will be loyal to the Messiah and hated of all nations for His name's sake. They will be hated and betrayed by their own people. They will constitute the remnant spoken of in such passages as Isaiah 10:20-23: "And it shall come to pass in that day, that the remnant of Israel, and such as are escaped of the house of Jacob, shall no more again stay upon him that smote them; but shall stay upon the LORD, the Holy One of Israel, in truth. The remnant shall return, even the remnant of Jacob, unto the mighty God. For though thy people Israel be as the sand of the sea, yet a remnant of them shall return: the consumption decreed shall overflow with righteousness. For the Lord God of hosts shall make a consumption, even determined, in the midst of the land."

The "consumption" referred to here is "a technical expression for the judgments preceding Messiah's reign," according to Darby, of which we hear so much in the Olivet discourse. It is during that time that the remnant will preach the gospel of the kingdom in all the world for a witness unto all nations, and "then shall the end come."

The word rendered "end" in Matthew 24:3 is quite different from the same word in verses 6, 13, and 14. The former is properly rendered "consummation" in the better translations. In order to distinguish it from the word used in verses 6, 13 and 14, the latter may be translated as "conclusion." Or one may be thought of as a culmination, and the other as a completion.

In neither case should it be thought that these words refer to just a moment or an hour or even a day. If the "consummation of the age" (v. 3) refers to the last, or seventieth, week of Daniel, then it will last at least seven years. But I believe the end referred to in Matthew 24:14 has to do with the termination of that period.

In dark contrast to the witness of the remnant of Israel among all nations at that time, there will be the most awful apostasy, here referred to as the placing of the abomination of desolation in the holy place.

The very mention of the holy place implies that there will be a religious center, recognized as such. To apply this to any place of Christian worship in this present time is to ignore the plain teaching of the New Testament concerning the church. According to it, the true church has no particular place on earth which is called the holy place as distinguished from all other holy places.

But the nation Israel did have such a place in the tabernacle, and later in the temple. Moreover, the Lord's reference to Daniel's prophecy here should settle it once and for all that He was speaking of the holy place with reference to Daniel's people and his holy city (cf. Dan 9:24).

There are two references to "the abomination that

maketh desolate" in the book of Daniel (11:31; 12:11). The word used for "abomination" in both places is the same word used with references to idols in 1 Kings 11:5, 7 and 2 Kings 23:13. Such, no doubt, is the meaning in Daniel's prophecy also.

Matthew 24:15 does not tell who it is that will set up this abomination or idol, but Daniel (7:25) tells of a character who will be very prominent in the time of the end. Judging from the description given of him there, he is the same one as in Revelation 13:1-8, commonly known as "the first beast."

But there is another beast mentioned in that same chapter (vv. 11-17), commonly known as "the second beast," who will say to them which dwell on the earth that "they should make an image to the beast, which had the wound by a sword, and did live." This second beast has power to give life, or breath, "to the image of the beast, that the image of the beast should both speak, and cause that as many as would not worship the image of the beast should be killed."

Nothing could be more reasonable than to suppose that this image will be set up in the holy place, because "all that dwell upon the earth shall worship him, whose names are not written in the book of life of the Lamb" (Rev 13:8). Indeed, the placing of an image in any other holy place would have little or no significance for a Jew.

The holy place in the tabernacle, and later in the

temple, had nothing in it to represent deity. As a matter of fact, the law strictly forbade the making of any such thing (Ex 20:4-6). Thus one can see how such a procedure would be utterly shocking to a God-fearing Jew and how it will one day be a signal for flight.

Daniel says this abomination will be set up at the time the sacrifice is taken away (11:31; 12:11). The removal of the one occurs at the same time as the setting up of the other. Of course the sacrifices were not offered in the holy place, that is, inside the sanctuary proper. Therefore the one cannot be removed to make room for the other. Physically, it would be quite possible to continue the offering of sacrifices upon the altar in the court of the temple after the idol is set up in the holy place. But morally that would be impossible. Idolatry and the worship of the true God cannot go on together. The temple of God has no agreement with idols (2 Co 6:16; Eze 8:3-5).

All of this supposes, of course, that there will then be a place on earth which the Jews will recognize as the holy place. It is quite possible that provision for such a place will be made in the covenant which the Roman prince will confirm with the many. But since the Scripture does not say so, one cannot be absolutely sure.

There is one thing, however, which is certain: the time is approaching when sacrifices and oblations will again be offered. The fact that they will be "taken away" implies that. To spiritualize here is only to create an unnecessary difficulty. Just how a spiritual sacrifice could be taken away is unknown. And to apply this to the abolition of animal sacrifices after the death of Christ is to create an even greater difficulty.

The fact that the "taking away" is not referred to in Matthew 24:15 need not hinder one from assuming it, because it is included in the reference to the prophecy of Daniel. It is probably omitted in Matthew because it is not the taking away of the sacrifice and the oblation which is the sign of the time of the end, but the setting up of the abomination of desolation.

"Then let them which be in Judea flee into the mountains" (Mt 24:16). Note that the Lord does not refer to any other location in the world—not even to Rome. Attention in that day will be focused upon Jerusalem and Judea. It was said to Daniel, "Seventy weeks are determined upon thy people and upon thy holy city" (Dan 9:24).

It is still the custom in that land for men to spend time on the housetop. But the news of the setting up of an idol in the holy place might reach some while at work in the field. But neither the one taking his leisure on the housetop nor the one busy in the field will have time to stop for anything then. They will have to flee immediately in order to escape the consequences of refusing to worship the image.

It is moving indeed to note the Lord's expressed pity for those who are with child and those that give suck in those days. The implication is that no consideration will be shown them because of their delicate condition, nor because they have the care of helpless babes. History will repeat itself and "they shall fall by the sword: their infants shall be dashed in pieces, and their women with child shall be ripped up" (Ho 13:16). Usually such barbarities are associated with bygone ages. But current history shows that "the tender mercies of the wicked are cruel" (Pr 12:10). Thank God that His compassions fail not.

Another thing which relieves this otherwise dark picture is the Lord's exhortation to prayer. That which occasions all this misery will not be averted, but the time for it to take place may be so regulated in answer to prayer that the people will not have to flee in the wintertime when the cold would only add to their misery. Not only the season of the year but the very day of the week when all of this begins will be determined by Him who hears the cry of His own.

There is something very precious about that. Inasmuch as this concerns Jews who will again be under the law, their flight would be limited to a Sabbath day's journey (Ac 1:12) in case the idol were set up on that day. The powers that be in those days will not know why they will set a certain day in a certain season, but He who makes the wrath of man to praise Him (Ps 76:10) will cause them to do His will, and that in answer to the prayer of His elect.

"Then shall be great tribulation, such as was not since the beginning of the world to this time, no, nor ever shall be" (Mt 24:21). It will be so awful that it will threaten the existence of the whole human race. "Except those days should be shortened, there should no flesh be saved" (v. 22).

The possibility of anything like that was frankly doubted by some until the day of the atom and hydrogen bombs. The human race has wonderfully recovered again and again from horrible scourges and devastating wars. But today man lives in constant fear of being totally destroyed by the very instruments he has designed for his protection. All of which shows that he knows nothing at all about the one who still controls even that which He permits. And for the sake of the elect He has shortened or limited the number of the days of that great tribulation.

"Thus saith the LORD, As the new wine is found in the cluster, and one saith, Destroy it not; for a blessing is in it: so will I do for my servants' sakes, that I may not destroy them all. And I will bring forth a seed out of Jacob, and out of Judah an inheritor of my mountains: and *mine elect* shall inherit it, and my servants shall dwell there" (Is 65:8-9).

These are the elect who are referred to in Matthew 24:22, 24 and 31. Like the elect of this present age of grace, they will be the foolish things, the weak things, the base things, and the despised things (1 Co 1:27-28). But they will be chosen of God; and for their sakes and in answer to their prayers, He will show Himself strong in their behalf. "This also cometh forth from the LORD of hosts, which is wonderful in counsel, and excellent in working" (Is 28:29).

3

THE COMING OF THE SON OF MAN

MATTHEW 24:22-31

ONE OF THE INTERESTING THINGS about the Olivet discourse is the number of warnings it contains. As already seen, it opens with a warning against those who will come in the Messiah's name, saying, "I am the Christ" (Mt 24:5, RV). Another solemn warning is given in connection with the setting up of the abomination of desolation in the holy place. Unlike the first, this is a warning to flee when an idol is set up in the sanctuary itself, "standing where it ought not" (Mk 13:14).

The law of Moses strictly forbade the making of "any graven image" (Ex 20:4) as an object of worship. While it is true that Christians are also told to "flee from idolatry" (1 Co 10:14), no particular form of idolatry is singled out. But the abomination of desolation is an idol which will mark the very worst form of sacrilege because it will desecrate the holy place itself.

In this portion of Matthew is another warning. It appears that the Antichrist will seek to imitate the true Christ down to the last detail. Therefore he will use false prophets or forerunners who will say, "Lo, here is Christ, or there." No doubt a number of these will try to imitate John the Baptist, the forerunner of the true Christ. These things will probably go on concurrently with the deception mentioned in verses 4 and 5.

Note that this chapter does not present everything in chronological sequence. For example, in verse 14 the Lord goes right on to "the end." But in the next verse He goes back again in point of time to something which takes place before "the end." The same is true in verse 22, because the shortening of the days of the great tribulation implies their termination. But in verse 23 He goes back again to speak of that which will characterize the time of the end.

The enemy's attempt to imitate the true Christ will be so complete that he will, no doubt, seek to simulate Christ's entry into the world, and also to perform miracles as He did. But though the Lord's forerunner did no miracles (Jn 10:41), it appears here that not only the false Christs but also their false prophets will perform such wonders. Their "coming is after [or, according to] the working of Satan with all power and signs and lying wonders, and with all deceivableness of unrighteousness in them that perish; because they received not the love of the truth, that they might be saved. And for this cause God shall send them strong delusion, that they should believe a lie [literally, the lie]: that they all might be damned who believed not the truth, but had pleasure in unrighteousness" (2 Th 2:9-12).

The imitation will be so clever that "if it were possible, they shall deceive the very elect." But the expression "if it were possible" implies that it will not be possible. The elect of that day will be protected from such a deception in the same way in which believers are protected today, by an unction from the Holy One (1 Jn 2:20).

It must not be thought that because the Holy Spirit will have completed His work of forming the church that He will then have nothing further to do. The Lord will pour His Spirit upon His ancient people Israel so that when they look upon Him whom they pierced they will recognize Him and mourn because of Him (Zec 12:10). And that same blessed Spirit will be their protection then, no matter how clever may be the enemy's attempt to deceive. Moreover, they will have the warning of the Lord Jesus Himself, who said, "Behold, I have told you before." To be forewarned is to be forearmed.

But the enemy will carry his imitation still further. He knows full well that the true Christ was "led up of the Spirit into the wilderness to be tempted of the devil" (Mt 4:1). Accordingly, when he presents his counterfeit, he will seek to imitate even the temptation. At any rate that would seem to be the purpose in the announcement, "Behold, he is in the desert."

In the reference to the "secret chambers" is detected a subtle reference to the Lord's own words when He said, "But thou, when thou prayest, enter into thy closet" (Mt 6:6). The word "closet" is the same word translated "secret chambers" here. It is used only four times in the New Testament, but it is translated by three different words. In Matthew 6:6 and Luke 12:3 it is rendered "closet," suggesting a place closed in, and thus shut off from all outside interference. In Luke 12:24 it is rendered "storehouse," suggesting a place of supplies. But here it is rendered "secret chambers," suggesting a place of privacy and security.

All of these are needed to give the full meaning of the original word. And one can readily see how attractive such a place would be in a time of tribulation and anguish. The very idea of an asylum or place of refuge will certainly have its appeal then. And the promise of finding one there who might give comfort and relief would only serve to heighten the desire to go out and find him.

Time was when men were able to search out the true Messiah in the desert or secret chambers. But that day has passed except, of course, as we still talk of finding the Lord in solitude. When He comes again as Son of man it will not be to repeat the experiences of the first advent. When He comes to judge the world, He will come as "the lightning cometh out of the east, and shineth even unto the west." Scripture nowhere speaks of the Lord's coming for His church in this manner. Lightning is something which is constantly associated with judgment in Scripture. And that is the way it should be understood here.

Moreover, the Lord's reference to the carcass, or corpse, is out of keeping with what He would be expected to say of His church, which is His body. In direct contrast to that living organism, a dead corrupt thing is here which will attract the birds of prey. Job speaks of "the eagle which hasteth to its prey" (9:26). And in the book of Habakkuk the eagle is associated with beasts of prey, such as leopards and wolves (1:8). These refer, from the immediate context, to that "bitter and hasty nation," the Chaldeans. No doubt the Lord is also referring here to some great power or powers that will swoop down upon the corrupt mass of His ancient people to whom He refers as the carcass.

It is at this time that the greatest blackout ever known will take place. "Immediately after the tribulation of those days shall the sun be darkened, and the moon shall not give her light, and the stars shall fall from heaven." These words remind us of the Lord's words to Pharaoh as recorded in Ezekiel

32:7-8: "When I shall put thee out, I will cover the heaven, and make the stars thereof dark; I will cover the sun with a cloud, and the moon shall not give her light. All the bright lights will I make dark over thee, and set darkness upon thy land, saith the Lord GOD." But in Matthew 24 we get something which is not mentioned in the word to Pharaoh: "The powers of the heavens shall be shaken."

The reference to these powers shows that something more than physical changes is involved. These powers are the same ones mentioned in Ephesians 6:12. They are already "spoiled" (Col 2:15), and the Lord has "made a show of them openly." But the time is coming when He will expel them altogether from the heavenly places which they now occupy, and "cast them down to hell" (2 Pe 2:4).

When the Lord comes for His church He will invade their present domain. It is "in the air" that He will meet His own (1 Th 4:13 ff.), and Satan is the prince of the power of the air (Eph 2:2). But the powers of the heavens will not be shaken at that time. Nevertheless, the Lord will not only enter their domain but will make of it a trysting place with the church for which He died. First, however, on the occasion described in verse 29, He will deal with these wicked powers. Having "shaken" them, He will then appear in the heavens, where every other light has been darkened, as if to clear the stage of

anything which might in any way seek to rival Him
in His glory.

"Then shall appear the sign of the Son of man in
heaven: and then shall all the tribes of the earth
mourn," just as Zechariah predicted long ago. The
fact that "tribes" are mentioned here probably means
that this is a special reference to that people which
is so well known for its tribal divisions. The reason
for their mourning is not given in Matthew 24, but
Zechariah 12:10 says that it is because they will
then look upon Him whom they pierced and will
recognize Him as the Messiah whom they rejected
long before.

Then shall they "mourn for him as one mourneth
for his only son, and shall be in bitterness for him as
one that is in bitterness for his firstborn." It has been
pointed out that here are two names which refer
most appropriately to our blessed Lord, who is not
only the unique Son of God but also the Firstborn
from among the dead.

Another thing which shows that this is not His
coming for the church is the fact that "he shall send
his angels . . . and they shall gather his elect from
the four winds, from one end of heaven to the
other" (v. 31). When He comes for His church, He
will not make use of such agencies to gather His
own to Himself. First Thessalonians 4:16 plainly
says that "the Lord himself shall descend from
heaven" to summon His own to meet Him "in the

air." In Matthew 24:31 there is not even a hint that
He will then remove His elect from the earth to
heaven.

It should also be noted that there is no reference
to the resurrection of the dead in Matthew 24:31,
whereas the resurrection of the dead in Christ is
one of the outstanding features of the Lord's coming
for His church. As a matter of fact, there is no
reference to the resurrection of the dead anywhere
in the Olivet discourse. That a matter so important
should be completely omitted from a detailed description of His coming as the Son of man constitutes
first-class proof that this passage does not deal with
what is commonly called the rapture.

Here is the gathering of an earthly people. But
they are no less His elect on that account. They are
referred to three times as such in this discourse. In
verse 22 they are called "the elect" for whose sake
He is going to shorten or limit the length of the
time of the tribulation. In verse 24 they are referred
to in the Authorized Version as "the very elect,"
whom it will be impossible to deceive just because
they are that. Finally, they are referred to as "his
elect."

In these three references three stages of true love
are seen. To begin with, the bride-to-be is "the elect,"
chosen from among all others as "the one and only."
Then comes the formal engagement when she be-

comes "the very elect." Finally, on the wedding day she becomes "his elect."

Thus it will be when the Lord takes up His ancient people again. He will open His eyes upon them in love (Zec 12:4), just as He did in the case of Peter (Lk 22:61). And when she, like Peter, is melted by that look of love, then He will speak comfortably unto her, saying, "Fear not, for I am with thee: I will bring thy seed from the east, and gather thee from the west; I will say to the north, Give up; and to the south, Keep not back: bring my sons from far, and my daughters from the ends of the earth; even every one that is called by my name: for I have created him for my glory, I have formed him; yea, I have made him" (Is 43:5-7).

Then she shall "no more be termed Forsaken . . . for the LORD delighted in thee, and thy land shall be married. For as a young man marrieth a virgin, so shall thy sons marry thee: and as the bridegroom rejoiceth over the bride, so shall thy God rejoice over thee" (Is 62:4-5).

Even though as Christians we do not have any direct part in all of this, yet we would pray:

> Lord, haste that day of cloudless ray,
>   That prospect bright, unfailing,
> Where God shall shine in light divine
>   In glory never fading.
>
> —F. WHITFIELD

4

THE FIG TREE AND ITS BRANCH

MATTHEW 24:32-35

THE FIRST MAJOR DIVISION of the Olivet discourse is concerned almost altogether with the dark side of things, such as deceit, treason, persecution and apostasy. But in this second portion is a bright and refreshing contrast. In it the Lord uses the familiar method of the parable to teach a lesson concerning His ancient people.

As Trench points out, "The parable, or other analogy to spiritual truth appropriated from the world of nature or man, is not merely illustration, but also in some sort [sense] proof. . . . They are arguments, and may be alleged as witnesses; the world of nature being throughout a witness for the world of spirit, proceeding from the same hand, growing out of the same root, and being constituted for that very end. All lovers of truth readily acknowledge these mysterious harmonies, and the force of the arguments derived from them."[1]

In the parable of the fig tree, the Lord uses a symbol which is quite familiar to the reader of the Old Testament. It was used by Jotham in the days of the judges (Judg 9:10-11). But the fig tree is mentioned much earlier than that in the Bible. It was in the Garden of Eden that our first parents sewed fig leaves together and made themselves aprons. The earliest use of the fig tree itself as a symbol of the Lord's people is found in Hosea 9:10: "I found Israel like grapes in the wilderness; I saw your fathers as the firstripe in the fig tree at her first time; but they went to Baal-peor, and separated themselves unto that shame."

In the prophecy of Jeremiah is a vision which that prophet had in which he saw two baskets of figs. "One basket had very good figs, even like the figs that are first ripe: and the other basket had very naughty figs, which could not be eaten, they were so bad" (Jer 24:2). The Lord Himself immediately gives the interpretation of this vision, saying, "Like these good figs, so will I acknowledge them that are carried away captive of Judah, whom I have sent out of this place into the land of the Chaldeans for their good. For I will set mine eyes upon them for good, and I will bring them again to this land: and I will build them, and not pull them down; and I will plant them, and not pluck them up."

Note that it is not the whole nation of Israel which is in view here, but only that part which was carried captive to Babylon by Nebuchadnezzar. In-asmuch as the ten tribes had been carried away to Assyria long before that, this must refer to the tribes of Judah and Benjamin, commonly known as the southern kingdom. But even though they were ac-tually taken captive by Nebuchadnezzar, the Lord says He sent them to Babylon for their own good. It is beautiful to note that He also promises to bring them back again to their own land.

The prophecy of Joel also refers to this. But there the nation into whose hands the Lord had delivered Judah is referred to as a "nation . . . strong, and without number, whose teeth are the teeth of a lion, and he hath the cheek teeth of a great lion. He hath laid my vine waste, and barked my fig tree: he hath made it clean bare, and cast it away; the branches thereof are made white" (Joel 1:6-7).

There are two things that should be noted partic-ularly here. On the one hand we have the vine, and on the other the fig tree and its branches. The vine, as we know from Isaiah 5 and Psalm 80, is a type of the nation of Israel as a whole. But in Isaiah 5:7 a distinction is made between "the house of Israel, and the men of Judah." The former is "the vineyard of the LORD of hosts," and the latter "his pleasant plant." Since the fig tree is noted for its pleasantness or sweetness (Judg 9:11), it is not difficult to see here a hint, at least, of the symbol used later to represent that part of the nation which was taken captive to Babylon.

In Luke 13:6 is another parable of the fig tree: "A certain man had a fig tree planted in his vineyard." In the light of Jeremiah 24:5-6, it seems quite clear that here is another reference to Judah brought back from Babylon and once more planted in the land.

Ezra likewise made reference to this restoration in his prayer when he said, "And now for a little space grace hath been shewed from the LORD our God, to leave us a remnant to escape. . . . For we were bondmen; yet our God hath not forsaken us in our bondage, but hath extended mercy unto us in the sight of the kings of Persia, to give us a reviving, to set up the house of our God, and to repair the desolations thereof, and to give us a wall in Judah and in Jerusalem" (Ezra 9:8-9).

It was to this remnant that Christ came seeking fruit. But He "found none" (Lk 13:6). And even though there was an extension of time granted (v. 8), the fruit for which He looked never appeared. Nevertheless, in the parable now before us He predicts a revival. And the fact that He used a fig tree and not a vine, seems to mean that the revival will begin in that part of the nation represented by the fig tree. Since "it is evident that our Lord sprang out of Juda" (Heb 7:14), it seems most appropriate that it should begin there.

In that connection it is of more than passing interest to note that He did not say "branches" but "his branch." It is only here and in the parallel passage (Mk 13:28) that we find the word "branch" in the singular in the New Testament.

Of all 'the men of Judah" there is only one of whom the Scripture speaks as "the Branch." In Isaiah 4:2 He is spoken of as "the Branch of the LORD," emphasizing His deity. But in Isaiah 11:1 we read that "a Branch shall grow out of his [Jesse's] roots," emphasizing His humanity.

Again in Jeremiah 23:5 the Lord says, "I will raise unto David a righteous Branch, and a King shall reign and prosper, and shall execute judgment and justice in the earth." Similarly, in Jeremiah 33:14, "Behold, the days come, saith the LORD, that I will perform that good thing which I have promised unto the house of Israel and to the house of Judah. In those days, and at that time, will I cause the Branch of righteousness to grow up unto David; and he shall execute judgment and righteousness in the land."

In Zechariah 3:8 the Lord refers to this same blessed one as His Servant "the Branch." Finally, in Zechariah 6:12-13 the Lord of hosts speaks, saying, "Behold the man whose name is The BRANCH; and he shall grow up out of his place, and he shall build the temple of the LORD; even he shall build the temple of the LORD; and he shall bear the glory, and shall sit and rule upon his throne; and he shall be a priest upon his throne: and the counsel of peace shall be between them both."

In Luke 21:29-30 no mention is made of "the branch." It reads, "Behold the fig tree, and all the trees; when they now shoot forth, ye see and know of your own selves that summer is nigh at hand." If this shooting forth refers to national revival, then there will not only be a revival of Israel as a nation but other nations which had special dealings with Israel in times past will also be revived. When we take into consideration what has been happening in such countries as Iraq, Iran and Egypt, we may well wonder if the time for such revival is drawing near.

But in Matthew and Mark there is more which has to do particularly with the Messiah. As already seen, He is "the Branch." And in the putting forth of leaves, I believe there is a revival of the Messianic hope, rather than the national revivals spoken of by Luke. It may well be that the latter will precede the former. But one must distinguish very carefully between that which is purely political and that which is spiritual.

No doubt some Jews even now are looking for the Messiah, but as a nation Israel does not look for Him. This was indicated in a news report of a conversation with one of the leading Jewish rabbis in the Chicago area, Dr. Edgar E. Siskin, of the North Shore Congregation Israel. According to that report,

"Reform Judaism does not believe in a coming Messiah, but looks forward to a Messianic age when humankind will turn from materialism to spirituality, love of God and love of all God's children."[2]

The present revival of nationalism in Israel is not a revival of the Messianic hope. Therefore it cannot be looked upon as a fulfillment of Matthew 24:32. But it might well lead up to it.

The recent publication of English translations of the Old Testament, by and for Jews especially, may be another indication that the spiritual revival is not far off. Scripture tells us that "blindness in part is happened to Israel, until the fulness of the Gentiles be come in" (Ro 11:25).

If, as some of us believe, there are indications that "the fulness of the Gentiles," that is, the complete number of the Gentiles to be saved, may come in at any time, then it will not be long before "all Israel shall be saved: as it is written, There shall come out of Sion the Deliverer, and shall turn away ungodliness from Jacob" (Ro 11:26). Then we shall know that summer (the millennium) is nigh. The winter (tribulation) will have passed and "the time of singing come." Then the fig tree will put forth her green figs, and the vines with the tender grapes will again "give a good smell" (Song 2:11-13).

It is when all of these things come to pass that it will be known "that it is near, even at the doors." According to the marginal reading in some editions of the Bible, this should read, "He is near." The Lord, however, had just spoken of the way in which they might know that summer is nigh. Therefore it seems more natural to look upon this as a reference to the time or season.

Christ's disciples asked Him when these things would come to pass (Mt 24:3). Among those "things" was His prediction that they, that is, the nation as a whole, would not see Him again until they should say, "Blessed is he that cometh in the name of the Lord" (Mt 23:39). In view of this, it may well be that this is one of those designed ambiguities of Scripture. Thus it may mean that "it [the season] is near," and "he is near." These statements are not contradictory; they are coalescent.

In direct connection with this, the Lord makes a statement concerning the nation of Israel itself which is most heartening. Taking into account the devastating effects of the great tribulation, one may well wonder if a small nation like Israel could possibly survive it. It is true that all through the centuries the Jews have survived persecution such as no other people has had to endure. And they have also resisted amalgamation with other peoples. But this will be different. Because of this, the Lord says, "Verily I say unto you, This generation shall not pass, till all these things be fulfilled" (v. 34). It is a matter of record that all attempts to exterminate them have failed. That generation, or race, is still here.

But these words have also been taken to mean that "the very generation that sees the beginning of these things will see the end."[3] In other words, these events will take place with such rapidity that all will be accomplished within one generation. And since a generation is generally reckoned to be about thirty years, that could easily be. In fact, it should not take even that long. And since this does not contradict the other view, it is quite possible that both meanings are included.

And the one who made this prediction says, "Heaven and earth shall pass away, but my words shall not pass away" (v. 35). What He says has more permanence than creation itself. "For ever, O LORD, thy word is settled in heaven" (Ps 119:89). What a privilege to see it fulfilled!

5

DIVINE DISCRIMINATION

MATTHEW 24:36-51

THE FIRST MAJOR DIVISION of the Olivet discourse deals particularly with doctrinal matters, especially those which relate to the person and work of Christ. This is seen at the very outset when the Lord Jesus issued a warning concerning those who would seek to impersonate Him, saying, "I am Christ." He also told His disciples that they—that is, those whom they represented then—would be hated of all nations for His name's sake. Again He warned them of false Christs and false prophets who would come, saying, "Lo, here is Christ, or there." And in the setting up of the idol known as "the abomination of desolation" is seen the climax of the apostasy.

Matthew 24:36-51 contains that which is moral rather than doctrinal, not that these two things can be separated. Good doctrine and good morals always go together. But we can distinguish what may not be separated.

Accordingly, notice that no further mention is made of those who will come in the name of Christ,

saying, "I am the Messiah." Neither are those mentioned who will be persecuted for His name's sake.
Here is the behavior of the just and the unjust, the
faithful and the unfaithful.

For an illustration of these things, the Lord went
back to the days of Noah. In so doing He incidentally
put His stamp of authentication on the biblical record of that cataclysm. But He did not go into detail.
To discover what it was that actually led to the judgment of the flood, one must go to the ancient record
itself. All the Lord says here is that the antediluvians
were eating and drinking, marrying and giving in
marriage, until the flood came and took them all
away. According to this, they were apparently
engaged in the normal and legitimate pursuits of
human beings.

But the ancient record, as given in the book of
Genesis, says that at that time the earth was filled
with violence and corruption. And not only that; in
their marrying and giving in marriage there was
grave irregularity, to say the least. If "the sons of
God" mentioned in Genesis 6 were those of the
human race whom the Lord acknowledged as His
children, it is clear why the Lord was provoked when
they intermarried with "the children of the wicked
one," namely, the line of Cain.

First John 3:12 plainly says that "Cain . . . was
of that wicked one, and slew his brother . . . because
his own works were evil, and his brother's righteous."

After that, when Seth was born, Eve said, "God . . . hath appointed me another seed instead of Abel, whom Cain slew." And, not long after that, "began men to call upon the name of the LORD." According to good authority, this might be rendered, "Then men began to call themselves by the name of the LORD." They would then be known as "the sons of God" to distinguish them from the line of Cain.

No doubt the two groups were kept quite distinct at the beginning. But in process of time the line of separation was no longer respected by the masses. There was, however, one outstanding exception. "Noah was a just man and perfect in his generations, and Noah walked with God" (Gen 6:9). As for the rest, "all *flesh* had corrupted his way upon the earth." "The wickedness of *man* was great in the earth." These and other references to flesh and to man all through this passage of Scripture show that it was human beings who were the offenders here.

The intermingling of the two lines, the children of God and the children of the wicked one, was followed by violence and corruption. It is ever thus. The children of God do not improve the world by mingling with it. On the contrary, they themselves are debased and corrupted by their departure from the divine principle of separation from evil.

At this point we may learn a lesson for our own times. It was not because of their eating and drinking that the Lord sent the flood upon man in the days of Noah. It was because of man's wickedness. "Every imagination of the thoughts of his heart was only evil continually." In thought, as well as in deed, man had become utterly wicked. And in spite of all of Noah's preaching (2 Pe 2:5), the men of his day "knew not until the flood came and took them all away." They had ample warning but they did not heed it. They went about their daily pursuits as if all were well, utterly indifferent to the preaching of righteousness which must certainly have condemned their whole way of life. Their ignorance was not the ignorance of innocence. It was deliberate and therefore culpable.

The Lord says that history will repeat itself, the truth of which can be seen on every hand today. If ever there was a time in the world's history which resembles the days of Noah, this is it. One has but to pick up his newspaper, or listen to the news reports over the radio, to confirm that. Truly the earth is filled with violence and corruption. And yet men go about their daily pursuits as if all this had no significance whatever.

When the Lord comes again as Son of man to judge the world, "then shall two be in the field; the one shall be taken, and the other left. Two women shall be grinding at the mill; the one shall be taken, and the other left." Only God can discriminate as finely as that. And if the illustration fits the case, as it certainly does, then those who are taken are taken in judgment, just as those who were taken in Noah's day were taken in judgment.

It has been argued against this view that the word for "taken" here is the same word which the Lord used in John 14:3 when He said that He would come again and "receive" us unto Himself, and that therefore Matthew 24:40-41 refers to the rapture.

But nothing is said in Matthew 24 about anyone being taken by the Lord "unto Himself." The verb in John 14:3 is in the middle voice, but in Matthew 24:40-41 it is in the passive voice. Moveover, the same word is used in Matthew 27:27, where we read that "the soldiers of the governor *took* Jesus into the common hall." It is similarly used of Paul in Acts 23:18. As a matter of fact, the Greek word *paralambano* is used nearly fifty times in the Greek New Testament, but usually the occurrences have nothing to do with the rapture or anything resembling it.

What happened in the days of Noah, however, should determine what is meant here. It was not Noah and his family who were *taken.* They were the ones who were *left.* All the while they were in the ark they never lost contact with the earth. In view of that, one fails to see how they can in any way represent those who will be raptured when the Lord comes for the church. It is Enoch, and not Noah, who gives us the illustration of what will take place when the Lord comes to receive His own unto Himself. "He was not, for God took him."

That is never said of Noah and his family, even
though Noah also walked with God.

Then, too, the fact that the Lord here draws a
parallel between His coming and that of a thief
shows that this does not refer to His coming for the
church. The day of the Lord will come as a thief in
the night. But we are not in darkness that that day
should overtake us as a thief (1 Th 5:2-4). When
the Lord comes for the church, it will not be to break
up His house (Mt 24:43) but to complete it. Thus
the illustrations which the Lord uses all through the
passage preclude the thought of any application of
these things to His coming for the church. But that
does not mean that there are no lessons for Christians
to learn from all of this.

As already seen, the Lord will have "his elect"
in that day. And it is beautiful to see how He makes
provision for them. The question in Matthew 24:45
rings out like a challenge: "Who then is a faithful
and wise servant, whom his Lord hath made ruler
over his household, to give them meat in due
season?"

In the midst of much unfaithfulness, such a servant will be outstanding. And the fact that he is commissioned to "give them meat in due season" shows
that the Lord is not unmindful of the needs of His
own in that day.

In contrast to those who will be "eating and drinking" without regard for others, or even for themselves,

this servant is set to feed the flock of God over which he has been made an overseer. And when the Lord comes and finds him "so doing," He will promote him to even higher honor. "He shall make him ruler over all his goods" (Mt 24:47). If we take the "goods" here to mean those treasures which are found in the Word of God, then it is evident what real force there is to the expression, "So-and-so has a great command of the Scriptures." Such "command" is the result not only of study but of faithful ministry to the Lord's own.

In dark contrast to this is "that evil servant" who shall say in his heart, "My Lord delayeth his coming." What a man says in his heart is what he thinks, and the wish is the father to the thought. The awful results of such thinking are seen in his conduct. He "shall begin to smite his fellow servants, and to eat and drink with the drunken." On the one hand he becomes antagonistic to his equals; on the other hand he finds his fellowship with those who, like the antediluvians, eat and drink, but in this case to excess.

"The Lord of that servant shall come in a day when he looketh not for him, and in an hour that he is not aware of." The Lord's coming will overtake him like a thief. And the judgment which will be meted out to him shows the class to which he belongs. The Lord "shall cut him asunder, and appoint him his portion with the hypocrites: there shall be weeping and gnashing of teeth."

The suddenness with which this judgment will come upon men is referred to several times in this portion of the Olivet discourse. In verse 36 the Lord says, "Of that day and hour knoweth no man, no, not the angels of heaven, but my Father only." In Mark 13:32 He even excludes Himself. "This the Lord's character as the Son of God in service sufficiently explains," says F. W. Grant. " 'The servant knoweth not what his lord doeth'. . . . It has been urged against this that it is not in this sense that no man or angel knoweth; but this as an objection has no force. For the point of our Lord's words is the inaccessibleness to *man* of this knowledge. There was none to whom one could go for this knowledge; neither man nor angel could communicate it, nor the Son either, as the apostle of His Father's will."[1]

When the Lord was asked by His disciples if He would at that time restore again the kingdom to Israel, He replied by saying that it was not for them to know "the times or the seasons which the Father hath put in his own power" (Ac 1:6-7). Thus, it is obviously the special function of the Father to set the times and the seasons. But the Spirit and the Son also have special functions. When we think of regeneration, we naturally think of the Holy Spirit. And when we think of redemption, we just as naturally think of the Son of God. As it is the prerogative of the one to regenerate, and of the other to redeem, so it is the prerogative of the Father to set the times and the seasons. And in this portion is seen the application of that to the coming of the Lord as the Son of man to judge the world.

Two exhortations are connected with that: "Watch therefore: for ye know not what hour your Lord doth come" and "Therefore be ye also ready: for in such an hour as ye think not the Son of man cometh."

To watch means not only to be observant but also to keep vigil and to be on one's guard. In view of all the evil that is around, how needful is such an exhortation. But they are also told to be ready, which means that they are to be completely prepared for what is going to happen then.

These exhortations we may well take to ourselves. We, too, need to be on our guard lest the enemy take advantage of us, and so much the more as we see the day approaching.

"Ye are all the children of light, and the children of the day: we are not of the night, nor of darkness. Therefore let us not sleep, as do others; but let us watch and be sober . . . putting on the breastplate of faith and love [to protect our hearts]; and for an helmet, the hope of salvation [to protect our minds]. For God hath not appointed us to wrath, but to obtain salvation by our Lord Jesus Christ, who died for us, that, whether we wake or sleep, we should live together with him" (1 Th 5:5-10).

6

THE TEN VIRGINS

MATTHEW 25:1-13

THIS PART OF THE WORD OF GOD presents a similitude of the kingdom of heaven which is peculiar to Matthew's gospel. Since it has no parallel in the other gospels, there is no opportunity to make comparisons which might help in the interpretation. That is probably one reason there is some diversity of opinion as to its meaning. Some commentators are quite sure that it refers to the church, whereas others are equally positive that it does not.

Some of the difficulty connected with the interpretation of this passage is due to the fact that some consider the church and the kingdom of heaven as one and the same thing. But the kingdom of heaven was in existence before the church. King Nebuchadnezzar had to learn that "the heavens do rule" (Dan 4:26). Even earlier than that the psalmist sang, "The kingdom is the LORD'S: and he is the governor among the nations" (Ps 22:28).

In this present age the church is part of the kingdom of heaven. However, the Lord is never referred to as the King of the church, but rather as its Head. If the Olivet discourse concerns events which will not take place until after the church has been removed from the earth, it is difficult to see how this passage could refer to the church unless it is taken out of its sequence here. On the other hand, the connective "then" seems to link it quite naturally with the preceding chapter. That is the way that we propose to treat it in this study.

The fact that the kingdom of heaven is here likened to ten virgins going forth to meet the bridegroom has led some to conclude that this is a positive similitude of Christ and the church. But observe that no mention is made of the bride. Even if she were mentioned, remember that the term is also used in Isaiah 62:5 to refer to the city of Jerusalem. And from the context there it seems clear enough that it refers to a day when Israel shall be restored, and when she shall "no more be termed Forsaken," neither shall her land anymore be termed desolate, for her land "shall be married. For as a young man marrieth a virgin, so shall thy sons marry thee: and as the bridegroom rejoiceth over the bride, so shall thy God rejoice over thee."

In harmony with this, John the Baptist refers to the Lord Jesus as the Bridegroom (Jn 3:29). But John suffered martyrdom before the Lord Jesus ever made the prophecy concerning the building of His church (Mt 16:18). Since that truth was not made

known in other ages (Eph 3:5-10), John obviously
was not referring to the Lord in His relationship to
the church when he referred to Him as the Bridegroom.

The Lord Jesus also referred to Himself as the
Bridegroom (Mt 9:15; Lk 5:34-35). But, strangely
enough, He is not referred to as such in the New
Testament epistles. Neither is the term *bride* used
in the epistles. Not until the book of Revelation
is it used again. There the prophet John was carried
away in the spirit to a great and high mountain and
was shown "the bride, the Lamb's wife . . . that great
city, the holy Jerusalem, descending out of heaven
from God" (21:9-10). In Galatians 4:25-26 the
apostle Paul contrasts the "Jerusalem which now is"
and the "Jerusalem which is above." He refers to the
latter as "the mother of us all," or as "our mother"
(literal Greek). But that does not mean that the
"Jerusalem which is above" is the same thing as the
church.

In any case, as noted, the bride is not mentioned
in Matthew 25. That the Bridegroom is the Lord
Jesus should be clear from the passages to which we
have already referred. It should also be clear from
those passages that such is His relationship to Israel.
Then, of course, the unnamed bride would be none
other than Israel herself.

It is said that a forgiven and restored wife could
not be called either a virgin (2 Co 11:2-3) or a

bride. Notwithstanding, the same sovereign grace that took up Jerusalem when she was polluted in her own blood (Eze 16) can do as much again. He to whom she proved so unfaithful has promised to betroth her unto Himself forever in righteousness and faithfulness (cf. Ho 2:19-20). Her sins will be so completely put away that God Himself has said He will remember them no more. He will yet speak comfortably unto her saying, "Fear not; for thou shalt not be ashamed: neither be thou confounded; for thou shalt not be put to shame: for thou shalt forget the shame of thy youth and thou shalt not remember the reproach of thy widowhood any more" (Is 54:4).

The whole of the chapter from which this passage is taken should be read to get the full force of this. The day is coming when Israel shall greatly rejoice in Jehovah; her soul shall be joyful in her God and she will sing, "He hath clothed me with the garments of salvation, he hath covered me with the robe of righteousness, as a bridegroom decketh himself with ornaments, and as a bride adorneth herself with her jewels" (Is 61:10).

According to Weymouth's translation of Matthew 25, the virgins are the bridesmaids, or, to use the language of Psalm 45:14, "the virgins her companions that follow her." Earlier in that same psalm (v. 9) it is said to the royal Bridegroom, "Kings' daughters were among thy honorable women: upon

thy right hand did stand the queen in gold of Ophir."
To apply that to the church is to ignore the clear
teaching of Ephesians 3:5-10. To do so would be to
rob Israel of that which is rightly hers as well as to
deprive ourselves of the light which it sheds on the
passage being studied.

The ten virgins are divided into two groups. "Five
of them were wise, and five were foolish." The latter
were foolish because they "took no oil with them:
but the wise took oil in their vessels with their
lamps." The difference between the two hinges on
that one thing. But that one thing is very important.
Zechariah 4 reveals that the oil is a type of the Holy
Spirit (see also Ac 10:38; Heb 1:9). "If any man
have not the Spirit of Christ, he is none of his" (Ro
8:9).

As virgins they are the very symbol of moral pu-
rity. Moreover, the lamps they carry speak of testimony. But of what use is a lamp without oil? It
takes a crisis, however, to make the foolish virgins
aware of their lack. And it is a lack for which they
can blame no one but themselves.

According to Zechariah 12:10 there will be a
fresh outpouring of the Spirit after the church is
gone. Says Jehovah, "I will pour upon the house of
David, and upon the inhabitants of Jerusalem, the
spirit of grace and of supplications: and they shall
look upon me whom they have pierced, and they
shall mourn for him, as one mourneth for his only

son, and shall be in bitterness for him, as one that is in bitterness for his firstborn."

No doubt that outpouring will result in what is sometimes called a "revival." It is not difficult to see that such might be the result of the preaching of the "gospel of the kingdom" (Mt 24:14). "The love of many" will be stirred up by it, but unfortunately, as in the case of the professing church now, that same love "shall wax cold." While the Bridegroom tarries, all of the virgins slumber and sleep.

Then at midnight, when all is in darkness, a cry will be heard, "Behold the bridegroom." "For, behold, the darkness shall cover the earth, and gross darkness the people: but the LORD shall arise upon thee, and his glory shall be seen upon thee" (Is 60:2). And the preceding verse says, "Arise, shine; for thy light is come, and the glory of the LORD is risen upon thee." But even before that other calls are given to awake (see Is 51:17; 52:1). Presumably there will be some response to these calls such as that in Matthew 25:1, 7. But when the Bridegroom actually arrives, those who have no oil will be left behind while they go to purchase that which cannot be bought with money (Ac 8:18-20).

In the descriptions of the rapture, such as those in 1 Thessalonians 4:13-18 and 1 Corinthians 15:51-54, no reference is made to any such group. There are "the dead in Christ" and those "which are alive and remain," but there is no hint that some of them

are wise and some foolish. Consequently, there is no
confusion as in Matthew 25:8-10. The events
referred to in each case are quite distinct from one
another. Therefore it is obviously not the church,
nor any part of it, that is in view here.

As already suggested, these virgins are the ones
spoken of in Psalm 45:14 as those who will be
associated with Israel in a coming day. It is interesting to note in that connection that the 144,000 who
will stand with the Lamb on Mount Zion are also
described as virgins (Rev 14:1-4). These are those
whose love will not "wax cold" (Mt 24:12). It has
been suggested that they may be "the martyrs of the
period with which the prophecy in general has to
do."[1]

In the light of church history, it is not difficult to
see that there will be then, as now, those who are
wise (Dan 12:3) and those who are foolish. Apparently there was a time when the lamps of the
foolish were burning along with those of their more
prudent sisters. But just when the lamps were
needed, they were discovered "going out" (Mt 25:8,
ASV). The virgins' vain appeal for oil was met with
the advice to go buy. But while they went to buy,
the priceless opportunity of meeting the Bridegroom
passed, and they were left outside, shut out from
the bridal festivities and denied the blessing of being
called to the marriage supper (Rev 19:9). Whether
they failed of more than this is not known. They

came to the closed door of the banqueting house and the Bridegroom refused to recognize them.

The judgments pronounced upon the unprofitable servant and upon the "goats" are much more severe (Mt 25:28-30, 41-46). Since the foolish virgins had not misjudged their Lord, nor yet neglected to succor the King's "brethren," their case may be considered to be like that of a Christian who may lose his reward but not his soul (1 Co 3:15; 5:5).

Thus, may there not be a lesson here for us? Are we not awaiting the coming of the Lord? Most assuredly! But the foolish virgins were also waiting for the coming of the Bridegroom. Their folly did not consist in any neglect of that truth. Doctrinally they were as sound or fundamental as their prudent sisters. All had the same forms (lamps); all were expecting the same Person. Their folly consisted in that they "took no oil with them."

If that means they did not have the Holy Spirit at all, then, of course, we shall have to consider them as lost. "If any man have not the Spirit of Christ, he is none of his" (Ro 8:9). But if it means they were not filled with the Spirit, then we may well learn a lesson here ourselves, for we are exhorted to "be filled with the Spirit" (Eph 5:18).

In any case, let us take these things to heart and seek by God's grace to be like unto men that wait for their Lord (Lk 12:35-36), letting our light so shine that men may glorify our Father which is in heaven (Mt 5:16). May the Lord use this to stir us all up, that we may give diligence to make our calling and election sure so that an abundant entrance into the everlasting kingdom of our Lord and Saviour may be richly furnished unto us (2 Pe 1:5-11).

7

TALENTS, USED AND UNUSED

MATTHEW 25:14-30

THIS, LIKE THE PRECEDING PART of the Olivet discourse, is peculiar to Matthew's gospel. Even though it does resemble the parable of the pounds (Lk 19: 11-27), the two are quite distinct. In the case of the pounds, each received a like amount to trade with, and the gains varied according to the diligence of the trader. In this parable the number of talents granted to each was based upon the ability of the recipient. In the case of those who received the pounds, nothing is said about the ability of the recipient.

It would appear therefore that in one parable is an illustration of that which all of the Lord's servants have bestowed upon them in like amount, whereas in the other is that which varies according to the ability of the recipients. They have gifts differing according to the grace bestowed upon them (Ro 12:6). It should be added, however, that such gifts may differ in kind and quality, as well as in quantity.

According to Ephesians 4:8, it was when the Lord

ascended on high that He gave gifts unto men. In keeping with that, the Lord is presented here as "a man traveling into a far country, who called his own servants, and delivered unto them his goods."

This is not the only time the Lord is presented in this way in the gospels. Matthew 21:33 tells of "a certain householder, which planted a vineyard, and hedged it round about, and digged a winepress in it, and built a tower, and let it out to husbandmen, and went into a far country." When these husbandmen refused to yield the fruits to the servants of the householder, "he sent unto them his son, saying, They will reverence my son." But they cast out his son and killed him.

The Lord Jesus likened that to the stone which the builders rejected. As Christians we have no difficulty in seeing in all of that the rejection of the Lord Jesus. He was the one who was sent from the "far country" to receive the fruits for which Jehovah looked (Is 5:2). But He was cast out.

Again, Mark 13:34 tells of "a man taking a far journey, who left his house, and gave authority to his servants, and to every man his work, and commanded the porter to watch." Nothing is said about talents, pounds or goods. But there can be no question about what the Lord meant here.

None of these, however, is exactly like the parable in Matthew 25, except that each speaks of our Lord's departure from this world, and His present absence during which His servants have certain responsibilities committed to them. It is also interesting to note that whereas in the other parables to which we have referred there are instructions to be followed, in Matthew 25 no instructions are given. It is simply stated that He "called his own servants" or bondmen "and delivered unto them his goods."

The word translated "goods" is the same word used in Matthew 24:47 and denoted "one's belongings, possessions, personal property," by Souter. The same word is found in Luke 16:1 in connection with the steward who wasted his master's goods. Quite possibly there is some connection between the two passages.

In any case it is quite obvious that Matthew 25 is actually teaching stewardship. The talents do not represent an original endowment or natural talent. Since they were distributed according to each one's several, or particular, ability, they must represent something bestowed in addition to any natural ability.

The literal talent, of course, was a monetary unit like the pound, but of much greater value. To receive even one talent meant to receive a considerable sum. Therefore to have five talents bestowed upon one denoted a large measure of ability on the part of the recipient.

That this one was worthy of such an endowment is indicated by the fact that he was able to gain another five. When the day of reckoning came, he had ten talents to present. And he who had received the two talents likewise justified the confidence placed in him when he showed that he too had doubled the original deposit.

If these talents may be used as an illustration of the gifts which the ascended Lord has given unto men, then the five talents are suggestive of the five gifts mentioned in Ephesians 4:11, "He gave some, apostles; and some, prophets; and some, evangelists; and some, pastors and teachers."

It is only an exceptional individual, however, who would be capable of exercising all of these gifts. Perhaps the apostle Paul came as near to that as anyone might come. He was not only an apostle but also a teacher, and certainly an evangelist. And who can deny that he also showed all the marks of a true pastor? The care of all the churches came upon him. But there are not many like him.

According to this parable, it did not take the servant long to get started. There is good reason to believe from the order of the words in the original text that "straightway" or "immediately" here refers to the one who had received the five talents. The urge to use all that had been given him was upon him.

Ephesians 4:12 says that such gifts were to be used "for the perfecting of the saints, for the work of the ministry, for the edifying of the body of Christ."

Since the passage being studied refers to a dispensation subsequent to that of the church, we conclude that similar gifts will be given in connection with the preaching of the gospel of the kingdom. As a matter of fact, the apostles were chosen in the first place to preach the gospel of the kingdom (Mt 10:1-7). And it is not difficult to see how the remaining gifts might be used then as well.

If in the servant who received the five talents is seen an instance of one who is highly capable, it is quite possible that in the case of the one who received two talents is seen what is probably more common, such as the pastor and teacher. But like his more highly gifted brother, he also "traded with the same" and "also gained other two." So far as the degree of achievement is concerned, he is not behind the other. If we use that which has been given to us in this way, it is still possible to increase our usefulness to the Lord Jesus.

"But he that had received one went and digged in the earth, and hid his lord's money." Here is the case of one who expends much energy without profitable result. With the same effort he might have gained in like proportion as his fellow servants. But it was not a matter of energy or the lack of it, but a wrong judgment of his lord that accounts for his behavior.

"After a long time the lord of those servants cometh, and reckoneth with them." "He that had

received the five talents" was the first to come before
his lord, with the report that he had "gained beside
them five talents more." And he who had received
the two talents reported that he had "gained two
other talents beside them." Each had doubled the
original deposit. Both received the same commenda-
tion, word for word.

Though only bondservants or slaves to begin with,
they now become rulers over many things. In this
respect they remind one of the servant of Matthew
24:45-47, and it may be that this portion should be
read in the light of that. For example, it is not difficult to see how the giving of meat to the household
might correspond to the gift of the teacher and
pastor.

But the man who received the one talent had no
gain to report. Instead he made a harsh misjudgment
of his lord. He was bold enough to tell him that
he knew him to be a hard man, reaping where he
had not sowed and gathering where he had not
strewn. He was actually accusing his lord of making
gains where he had made no original investment.
But even the one talent which he had received was
a flat denial of that base charge. One wonders at
such words, especially in view of the fact that he says
right after that, "I was afraid."

Observe that when he referred to the talent he
spoke of it as "thy talent." He did not say, as did the
others, "which thou deliveredst unto me." He never

considered it a sacred trust as they did. And when he returned it to his lord, he said, "Lo, there thou hast that is thine." It is as if he actually despised the gift.

Accordingly, he was judged out of his own mouth. His lord described him as being both wicked and slothful and, after repeating his own words, said that he should have invested his money so that it might have earned interest.

He is condemned on two counts. Not only did he misjudge his master; but if he really thought his master was a hard man, he should have seen to it that his money was put to work. Having failed to make any use whatsoever of the talent, he had it taken from him and given to the one who had ten talents.

That shows that the master himself did not want his gift back. The whole suggestion to invest his money grew out of the awful statement which the servant had made about his master. That explains the severity of the judgment meted out to him. As an "unprofitable servant" he is cast "into outer darkness: there shall be weeping and gnashing of teeth."

A striking instance of this is seen in the case of Judas Iscariot. He, too, had been entrusted with a talent, having been chosen as an apostle. But he fell from that ministry and apostleship by transgression, in order that he might go to his own place (Ac 1:25).

No doubt he had committed to him the same

powers which the other apostles had. But he either misused them or else failed to use them at all. And, worst of all, he betrayed his Lord. Judging from the sad end to which he came, he no doubt went into the outer darkness.

Thus, on the one hand there is abundant reward; on the other, there is terrible loss. But the faithful servants not only retain all of their gains but they are also made rulers of many things. And besides all that, they enter into the joy of their Lord, the greatest compensation of all.

It is not explained just what that joy is. But if these talents are gifts to be used for the winning of souls and for the edification of the Lord's people, then certainly the joy of the Lord is that joy which is His when sinners repent and backsliders are restored to Him (Lk 15). It is to His restored people that the prophet says, "The LORD thy God in the midst of thee is mighty; he will save, he will rejoice over thee with joy; he will rest in his love, he will joy over thee with singing" (Zep 3:17).

Of course that very plainly refers to a time still future. But that does not mean that there are no lessons to learn from this for the present. How good to know, however, that our destiny does not depend on our faithfulness, as was the case under the law.

We are not under the law but under grace. But after the church is removed from this scene, we have reason to believe that the law of Moses will again be in force. Otherwise there would be no point to statements such as we find in Matthew 24:20.

It is a solemn thing to be entrusted with divine gifts in any age or dispensation, particularly in this age of grace. But the more we know of the grace of God, the less inclined we shall be to abuse it. The very prospect of entering into those joys and pleasures which are eternal (Ps 16:11) should serve to make us very diligent in the use of all that He has entrusted to us. "It is required in stewards, that a man be found faithful" (1 Co 4:2). And that is something which applies to all ages and dispensations.

Strictly speaking, however, the portion being considered has to do primarily with that age which will follow this age of grace. That there will be a ministry such as this at that time has already been seen in the study of Matthew 24:45-51. And that is confirmed by such passages as Isaiah 66:19-24 and Daniel 12:3.

Isaiah writes concerning the spared remnant of Israel, "I will send those that escape of them unto the nations . . . that have not heard my fame, neither have seen my glory; and they shall declare my glory among the Gentiles." And Daniel says, "They that be wise shall shine as the brightness of the firmament; and they that turn many to righteousness as the stars forever and ever."

Then, as now, men will be gifted for the tasks assigned to them by "the Lord of the harvest," but they will exercise those gifts under the law in keeping with the general character of that dispensation. And that accounts for the fact that "the unprofitable servant" is cast into outer darkness, where there will be weeping and gnashing of teeth.

There is something unspeakably solemn about that. But such judgment "is according to truth against them which commit such things" (Ro 2:2). By way of contrast, it is comforting to note that in that same day "whosoever shall give to drink unto one of these little ones a cup of cold water only in the name of a disciple, verily I say unto you, he shall in no wise lose his reward" (Mt 10:42).

8

THE SHEEP AND THE GOATS

MATTHEW 25:31-46

IN THE SECTIONS IMMEDIATELY PRECEDING THIS closing portion of the Olivet discourse, the Lord has been seen both as a bridegroom and as a businessman. In this last part we see Him as the Son of man coming in His glory, accompanied by all of the holy angels. And "then shall he sit upon the throne of his glory."

At present He sits upon His Father's throne (Rev 3:21), "on the right hand of the Majesty in the heavens" (Heb 8:1); upon "the throne of grace" (Heb 4:16). The change to "the throne of his glory" indicates a change of dispensation. It indicates the taking unto Himself His "great power" (Rev 11:17). And even though no mention is made of the church in the Olivet discourse, Colossians 3:4 says that "when Christ, who is our life, shall appear, then shall ye also appear with him in glory."

Then shall all the nations be gathered before Him. Presumably these nations are Gentiles as distin-

guished from the Jews. It is in this way that the
term *nations* is commonly used in the Scriptures.
But observe that these are living nations. Nothing
is said here about the resurrection of the dead. As a
matter of fact, there is no reference to the resurrection of the dead anywhere in the Olivet discourse.
The events described therein have to do with those
living on the earth at that time, and not with those
who have died.

Then shall He who knows the hearts of all men
"separate them one from another, as a shepherd
divideth his sheep from the goats." This reference
to the practice of a shepherd is most interesting. In
the Old Testament the Messiah is often presented as
a shepherd. The Shepherd of Psalm 23 is the King
of glory of Psalm 24. In Psalm 80, He is the Shepherd of Israel enthroned between the cherubim. And
in Ezekiel 34:12 the Shepherd Himself says, "As a
shepherd seeketh out his flock in the day that he is
among his sheep that are scattered; so will I seek out
my sheep, and will deliver them out of all places
where they have been scattered in the cloudy and
dark day." Even though these passages speak particularly of His relationship to His ancient people
Israel, nevertheless they do not preclude the idea of
a similar relationship to others as well.

Having divided the nations into two groups, He
now assigns them their places, "the sheep on his
right hand, but the goats on the left." The right

hand is the place of honor (Ps 45:9; 110:1). When Jacob put his right hand upon the head of Ephraim, he was honoring him above his brother Manasseh (Gen 48:9-20). But in this case, the goats are not merely secondary to the sheep; they stand out in contrast to them. Since both sheep and goats are clean animals according to the law of Moses, why would the goats be used in contrast to the sheep?

It is quite possible that here the goats stand for those who outwardly profess to be righteous. That would be in keeping with what they would naturally claim for themselves. Outwardly they wear the clothing of a clean animal but "inwardly they are ravening wolves" (Mt 7:15).

He who sees not as man sees, however, is well able to penetrate that disguise. In Ezekiel 34:17 we hear Him saying, "As for you, O my flock, thus saith the Lord GOD; Behold, I judge between cattle and cattle, between the rams and the he goats." These "he goats" are also referred to in Isaiah 14:9 as "the chief ones of the earth," the same Hebrew word being used in both places. They are evidently leaders who have abused the flock (see Eze 34:18-22).

In the passage being studied, however, the emphasis is upon their neglect of a group whom the King refers to as His "brethren." Failure to distinguish this third group has led to much confusion in the interpretation of this portion of the Word. And yet it is perfectly plain that they are distinct from both the sheep and the goats. Everything here hinges on the treatment which they received, or failed to receive, as the case might be.

Note first of all that in addressing those on His right hand, the King refers to them as the blessed of His Father for whom a kingdom has been prepared ever since the world was founded. What the Lord is about to do now is no afterthought; it was His forethought. It was as sure when He purposed it as if it had been already accomplished. No power, however great, can thwart His purpose. The intervening centuries are but an episode. A thousand years in His sight are but as yesterday when it is past, and as a watch in the night (Ps 90:4).

All the purposes of God revolve around and center in His Son and, incidentally, those who are identified with His Son. It is touching to hear the King refer to the latter as His "brethren," and to their distress as His own. "In all their affliction he was afflicted" (Is 63:9). He says to those on His right hand, "I was an hungered, and ye gave me meat: I was thirsty, and ye gave me drink: I was a stranger, and ye took me in: naked, and ye clothed me: I was sick, and ye visited me: I was in prison, and ye came unto me."

But those who did these things were altogether unaware of the implications of their deeds. To their great surprise, they learn that what they had done was received by the Lord Jesus as if it had been done to Him personally. The actual recipients, of course, are those whom the Lord here acknowledges as His "brethren," who will be hated of all nations, not merely because they are Jews but for His name's sake (Mt 24:9-10). Any act of kindness shown to them in that day will put the benefactor "on the spot." But to visit such in prison will require unusual courage. Perhaps that is why it is mentioned last here as being the greatest service that might be rendered.

In that connection it is interesting to see how much the apostle Paul appreciated such a visit. Speaking of one who befriended him when he was in prison, he says, "The Lord give mercy unto the house of Onesiphorus; for he oft refreshed me, and was not ashamed of my chain: but, when he was in Rome, he sought me out very diligently, and found me" (2 Ti 1:16-17). It was the same Paul who, having learned that he was persecuting Jesus (Ac 9:5) when he was persecuting and ravaging the church (Gal 1:13), was now learning from personal experience how close is the bond that exists between the Lord and His own. It is very precious to note that this applies to "the least" of His brethren.

By way of contrast, we now hear the King saying to those on His left hand, "Depart from me, ye cursed." But He does not add "of my Father." Neither does He say that they have been cursed "from the foundation of the world." The blessing for those on His right hand was prepared long before.

Not so the curse pronounced upon those on His left hand. The place to which they are committed was not prepared for them but for "the devil and his angels." How unspeakably solemn that men should have to share the devil's destiny!

If it were merely a question of the way in which one human being had treated another, we might well wonder at the severity of the judgment here meted out. But, as already noted, those so condemned are evidently leaders who have posed as righteous men, but who satisfied their own lusts at the expense of the "brethren" of the King.

The gravity of an offense is measured by the dignity of the person offended. And even the least of these His brethren must be a prince. It should be quite evident that the sin for which those on His left hand are condemned is not one of ignorance but of willful neglect. And that accounts for the severity of the judgment.

Nevertheless, the "goats" demand an explanation. They want to know when they saw Him in distress of various kinds and did not minister to Him. His reply is, "Verily I say unto you, Inasmuch as ye did it not to one of the least of these, ye did it not to me." Just why the Lord did not add "my brethren" is not known, but He certainly was referring to the very same persons mentioned in verse 40. No matter how insignificant they may appear in the eyes of men, they are precious in His sight.

From the last verse of the chapter, which is also the end of the discourse, is learned that the issues involved are eternal. There is no difference in meaning between the words here rendered "everlasting" and "eternal." They represent the same word in the original Greek. And since the same word is used in speaking of "the everlasting God" (Ro 16:26), there can be no question at all about its true meaning.

But even though the issues here involved are eternal, this judgment must not be confused with that of the great white throne. That will not take place until a thousand years later (Rev 20:5, 11-15). Moreover, it will concern the dead, not the living. It is then that the dead will be judged out of those things which were written in the books, according to their works.

Before that, two will be cast alive into the lake of fire burning with brimstone (Rev 19:20). That will occur when "the Son of man shall send forth his angels, and they shall gather out of his kingdom all things that offend, and them which do iniquity; and shall cast them into the furnace of fire: there shall be wailing and gnashing of teeth. Then shall the righteous shine forth as the sun in the kingdom of their Father" (Mt 13:41-43).

Thus the Olivet discourse takes us to the very close or consummation of the (Jewish) age which will usher in the millennium, when the priests of God and of Christ shall reign with Him a thousand years. And that concludes the Lord's answer to those questions asked Him "as he sat upon the mount of Olives" (Mt 24:3).

There are many indications that the time for these things to be fulfilled is near at hand. That should have a sobering effect upon all of us. Our hope and prayer is that our study of them may result in greater devotion to our blessed Lord and greater diligence in His service.

9

THE PROPHECIES OF MARK 13
AND LUKE 21

IN COMPARING Mark 13 and Luke 21 with Matthew 24, certain interesting and significant differences can be noted. Of course, some persons would use these differences as arguments against the verbal inspiration of Holy Scripture. But while the fact that the accounts do differ is not denied, some of these differences are easily accounted for by taking into consideration the fact that each writer had a distinct purpose in mind (see Lk 1:1-4). Moreover, the differences are not contradictions; they consist mainly in omissions and additions.

First, both Matthew and Mark name the place at which the Lord uttered these prophecies. Because of this, they have been given the collective name of the Olivet discourse. Luke does not mention the Mount of Olives, but it is quite possible that what he records was actually spoken by the Lord before He took His seat on the Mount of Olives. The opening verses of Luke 21 show that the Lord was at or near the treasury. And verse 5 makes it appear that those who spoke "of the temple, and how it was adorned with goodly stones and gifts" were actually in the temple area at that time. Luke does not say who the "some" were. He does not even identify them as disciples of the Lord Jesus, even though their questions were quite similar to the questions raised by the disciples, as noted by Matthew (24:3) and Mark. Indeed, Mark even names them, saying, "As he sat upon the mount of Olives over against the temple, Peter and James and John and Andrew asked him privately, Tell us, when shall these things be?" (Mk 13:3-4). But Mark does not include the two questions recorded by Matthew, namely, "And what shall be the sign of thy coming, and of the end of the world [or, consummation of the age]?" In both Mark and Luke the questions are limited to the stones and the buildings of the temple. Nothing is said about the Lord's coming or the consummation of the age.

Our Lord's answer to these questions also has important distinctions. In Matthew 24:5, He says, "Many shall come in my name, saying, I am Christ; and shall deceive many." But in Mark and Luke we read that He said, "Many shall come in my name, saying, I am." The translators of the Authorized Version added the word "Christ" to make these passages conform to Matthew 24:5. But the word "Christ" does not appear in the original of Mark 13 or Luke 21. Since many will be coming in His name, it is not difficult to see how some would emphasize the Messiahship of the one whom they claim to be, and some His deity.

The mention of wars and rumors of wars in all three of these passages may mean nothing more than that such things will characterize every generation till the Prince of peace comes to put a stop to them. It is clear from Matthew 24:6 that they are not a sign of the end. In spite of that clear statement, many still think that they are a sign of the end.

We know from Daniel 9:27 that the beginning of "the time of the end," or the seventieth week of Daniel, will be marked by the confirmation of a covenant between a Roman prince and the mass of the Jewish people. I believe their being delivered up to tribulation (Mt 24:9) refers to that event. But in Mark and Luke the Lord merely speaks of their being delivered up to the Sanhedrin, and to their being beaten in synagogues. In other words, He prepares them for what they were to receive at the hands of their own countrymen for Christ's sake. The book of Acts gives several examples of that. One is, "As they spake unto the people, the priests, and the captain of the temple, and the Sadducees, came upon them, being grieved that they taught the people, and preached through Jesus the resurrection from the dead. And they laid hands on them, and put them in hold unto the next day: for it was now eventide" (Ac 4:1-3). After a so-called trial, "they called them, and commanded them not to speak at all nor teach in the name of Jesus" (v. 18). What the Lord predicted in Mark 13:9 and Luke 21:12 had already come to pass.

When their persecutors asked them by what power or by what means they had healed a lame man (Ac 3), "Peter, filled with the Holy Ghost, said unto them, Ye rulers of the people, and elders of Israel . . . be it known unto you all, and to all the people of Israel, that by the name of Jesus Christ of Nazareth, whom ye crucified, whom God raised from the dead, even by him doth this man stand here before you whole. This is the stone which was set at naught of you builders, which is become the head of the corner. Neither is there salvation in any other: for there is none other name under heaven given among men, whereby we must be saved" (Ac 4:7-12). By comparing this with 1 Corinthians 15:1-3 it is apparent that this is the same gospel that Paul preached. In that connection, note that neither Mark nor Luke mention "the gospel *of the kingdom*," as does Matthew. The terms of that gospel are clearly set forth in Matthew 10:7-15.

The reference to the Holy Spirit in Mark 13:11 also marks an important difference between Mark's writing and that reported in Matthew 24, where the Holy Spirit is never mentioned. This does not mean, of course, that the Holy Spirit will not have a part in the ministry of the gospel of the kingdom, for

Zechariah 12:10 says there will be a fresh outpouring of the Spirit on the house of David and the inhabitants of Jerusalem at that time. But Matthew makes no reference to that. Luke quotes this statement of our Lord earlier in another context (Lk 12:12). Moreover, the promises given in Mark 13:11 and Luke 21:14-15 are not found in Matthew 24:14. The preaching referred to by Matthew will be brought to an abrupt end by the setting up of the abomination of desolation (Mt 24:15), something to which Luke does not refer at all. He is concerned with a ministry which antedates that (Lk 21:12).

The promise given in Luke 21:14-15 is very precious: "Settle it therefore in your hearts, not to meditate before what ye shall answer: for I will give you a mouth and wisdom, which all your adversaries shall not be able to gainsay nor resist." This promise was literally fulfilled in the case of Stephen as he stood before the Sanhedrin: "And they were not able to resist the wisdom and the spirit by which he spake" (Ac 6:10). Even earlier than that "when they saw the boldness of Peter and John, and perceived that they were unlearned and ignorant men, they marvelled; and they took knowledge of them, that they had been with Jesus" (Ac 4:13).

In Luke 21:20-24 there is something else which is peculiar to Luke—a prophecy concerning the destruction of Jerusalem which is not found in Matthew or Mark. But Daniel had been told long before

that "the people of the prince that shall come" were
to destroy the city and the sanctuary (Dan 9:26).
According to Luke 21:24, that destruction was to be
followed by the treading down of the city until the
times of the Gentiles are fulfilled.

The times of the Gentiles will not be terminated
by a precarious occupation of Jerusalem. Rather,
they will be brought to a definitive close by the falling of the stone "cut out of the mountain without
hands" (Dan 2:45). In Nebuchadnezzar's dream
"the stone that smote the image became a great
mountain, and filled the whole earth," representing
"the kingdom [that] shall not be left to other people." "It shall stand for ever." The King of that
kingdom is the one whom the Lord recognizes as
His King (Ps 2:6). All He needs to do is to ask and
He will be given the heathen for His inheritance,
and the uttermost parts of the earth for His posses-
sion. And He "shall break them with a rod of iron"
and "dash them in pieces like a potter's vessel" (Ps
2:8-9). That will end the times of the Gentiles.

What Luke writes after this is very similar to
Matthew 24 and Mark 13. But there are some interesting differences. For example, in Luke 21:28:
"And when these things begin to come to pass, then
look up, and lift up your heads; for your redemption
draweth nigh." The "things" referred to here are
those mentioned in verses 25 and 26. Then, in common with Matthew and Mark, he gives them a

happier sign by which they may know "that the kingdom of God is nigh at hand." It is the sign of "the fig tree." But in his presentation of this he includes "all the trees" and says, "When they now shoot forth, ye see and know of your own selves that summer is now nigh." Verse 31 makes clear what is meant by the "summer."

Concurrent with the spiritual revival of Israel there will be a political revival of those nations which were intimately related to Israel in other days. Until quite recently these nations were not mentioned very much in press dispatches. But today almost daily reference is made to Iraq (ancient Babylonia and Mesopotamia), and Iran (Persia), as well as Egypt, Greece, etc. The only one of the old empires that is not mentioned by name as yet is Assyria, which must not be confused with Syria. (An easy way to distinguish them is to remember that Nineveh was the capital of Assyria, whereas Damascus is the capital of Syria.) Because of the suddenness with which political changes take place these days, there is reason to believe that soon Assyria might rise again. Some persons in the United States even now want to be known as Assyrians. In a cemetery not far from Chicago there is a monument erected to the memory of such on which are carved the words, "We are Assyrians."

That Assyria will rise again is implied in the prophecies concerning it in the book of Isaiah: "It

shall come to pass, that when the Lord hath performed his whole work upon mount Zion and on
Jerusalem" that He will "punish the fruit of the
stout heart of the king of Assyria, and the glory of
his high looks" (Is 10:12). Since the Lord has not
as yet performed His whole work upon Mount Zion
and Jerusalem, it stands to reason that Assyria will
yet arise and be dealt with as predicted. "And it
shall come to pass in that day, that the remnant of
Israel, and such as are escaped of the house of Jacob,
shall no more again stay upon him that smote them;
but shall stay upon the LORD, the Holy One of Israel,
in truth" (Is 10:20).

The same chapter goes on to speak of the time
when the prophecies included in the Olivet discourse will be fulfilled. "For the Lord GOD of hosts
shall make a consumption, even determined, in the
midst of all the land. Therefore thus saith the Lord
GOD of hosts, O my people that dwellest in Zion,
be not afraid of the Assyrian: he shall smite thee with
a rod, and shall lift up his staff against thee, after
the manner of Egypt. For yet a very little while, and
the indignation shall cease, and mine anger in their
destruction" (Is 10:23-25).

It is Mark who tells us that the "very little while"
has already been shortened or limited "for the elect's
sake" (Mk 13:20). Except for that gracious shortening, the whole human race would be wiped out; "no
flesh should be saved." And yet, while all of this is

going on, there will be a ministry of the Holy Spirit as predicted in Zechariah 12:10 where the Lord says, "I will pour upon the house of David, and upon the inhabitants of Jerusalem, the spirit of grace and of supplications: and they shall look upon me whom they have pierced, and they shall mourn for him, as one mourneth for his only son, and shall be in bitterness for him, as one that is in bitterness for his firstborn." It has been pointed out that there are two comparisons in this verse which point to the one who is indeed the only Son as well as the Firstborn, in a unique sense. Truly, "the testimony of Jesus is the spirit of prophecy" (Rev 19:10). "Now there are diversities of gifts, but the same Spirit. And there are differences of administrations, but the same Lord. And there are diversities of operations, but it is the same God which worketh all in all" (1 Co 12:4-6).

10

THE LORD'S COMING IN JOHN

THERE IS NO DIRECT REFERENCE to the Olivet discourse in the gospel of John, but there are references to the fact that the Lord Jesus has had all judgment committed to Him because He is the Son of man, a title which occurs frequently in Matthew 24 and 25. A number of references to "the Son" are in John 5, but only one reference is to the Son of man, and that is found in connection with judgment (v. 27). It is as Son of man that He will call forth "all that are in the graves" (v. 28). Two resurrections are clearly distinguished in verse 29: "the resurrection of life" and "the resurrection of damnation." From Revelation 20:5 we learn that these two resurrections will be separated in time by a period of a thousand years.

It is the first of these resurrections that is referred to four times in John 6:39, 40, 44 and 54. These verses present first of all a divine act, and then a human act. In verse 39 the Lord says, "This is the Father's will which hath sent me, that of all which he hath given me I should lose nothing, but should raise it up again at the last day." There was but one exception to this, as is learned from John 17:12, "that the scripture might be fulfilled." It was when Judas Iscariot, that one exception, led forth a band to arrest the Lord that He said, "If therefore ye seek me, let these go their way: that the saying might be fulfilled which he spake, Of them which thou gavest me have I lost none" (Jn 18:8-9). Divine grace had given them to Him; He, by divine power, had kept them. And He will keep them to "the last day" when they shall enter into that which is life indeed.

In the next verse (40) is seen the human side of this: "And this is the will of him that sent me, that every one which seeth the Son, and believeth on him, may have everlasting life: and I will raise him up at the last day." The word for "seeth" in this verse means to observe or perceive. It is something more than a passing glance. Indeed, it may be thought of as a look of faith or of believing, with which it is connected in the same verse. This seeing and believing present the human side.

In verse 44 the Lord speaks of the Father drawing men to Him, saying, "No man can come to me, except the Father which hath sent me draw him." Here again is divine activity. Many of us can testify to the fact that He drew us most graciously, so we can sing with truth,

'Twas the same love that spread the feast
    That gently forced me in,
Else I had still refused to taste,
    And perished in my sin.

—ISAAC WATTS

John 6:54 tells what that feast is: "Whoso eateth my flesh, and drinketh my blood, hath eternal life; and I will raise him up at the last day. For my flesh is meat indeed, and my blood is drink indeed." That these words are to be understood in a spiritual sense is clearly indicated in verse 63 where the Lord says, "The words that I speak unto you, they are spirit, and they are life." Peter understood them to be so, for he said, "Thou hast the words of eternal life" (v. 68). It is by faith that believers feast upon His person and His work. But this is quite distinct from the Lord's Supper. When the Lord spoke these words, that supper had not been inaugurated. Moreover, this very chapter says eternal life is obtained by believing on Him (Jn 6:47). Unfortunately, there are those who "take communion" without ever having believed on Him. According to 1 Corinthians 11:29, they eat and drink judgment to themselves. For them there will also be a "last day" (Jn 12:48), but it will be a day of judgment. "The last day" referred to in John 6 will be a glad day which might well be the day when He comes again to receive believers unto Himself as He promised in John 14:1-3. There the emphasis is upon the fact that Christians shall

be with Him according to His own desire (Jn 17:
24). Beyond that blessed truth John's gospel does
not go. One more reference to His coming is in
John 21:22, but no details are given. For details one
must go to the epistles.

From the foregoing it is obvious that it was not
John's primary purpose to speak of the Lord's coming
in judgment, even though he does refer to it in
chapter 5. But he, under God, makes the first mention of the blessed hope.

11

THE LORD'S COMING IN ACTS

THE DOCTRINE of the coming of the Lord is not often referred to in the book of the Acts. When it is mentioned it has to do with Israel and the world, rather than with the church.

Immediately after the ascension of the Lord, two men in white apparel announced to His disciples that He would come again in like manner as they had seen Him go. Since they were then on "the mount called Olivet" (1:12), it would seem that the two men were speaking of that day when "his feet shall stand . . . upon the mount of Olives" (Zec 14:4). At any rate, that is in keeping with their interest in the restoration of the kingdom to Israel (Ac 1:6). They were actually representatives of the godly remnant of Israel rather than of the church, since Pentecost had not yet come. It was while He was blessing them that the Lord left them, and it will be in blessing that He will return when "he shall come down like rain upon the mown grass: as showers that water the earth" (Ps 72:6).

The prophet Ezekiel depicts His return as "the glory of the God of Israel" coming "from the way of the east: and his voice was like the sound of many waters; and the earth shined with his glory" (Eze 43:2, ASV). "And what is that but a prophecy in symbolic language of the same event which the heavenly messengers announced to the men of Galilee, that 'this same Jesus, which is taken up from you into heaven, shall so come in like manner as ye have seen Him go up into heaven.' And not only 'in like manner'—that is, bodily, visibly—but He shall come *to the same place* whence He finally departed."[1]

In Acts 2:20 Peter speaks of the coming of "that great and notable day of the Lord." In his quotation from the prophecy of Joel he says that God "will shew wonders in heaven above, and signs in the earth beneath; blood, and fire, and vapour of smoke: the sun shall be turned into darkness, and the moon into blood, before that great and notable day of the Lord come" (vv. 19-20). The Lord Jesus used similar language when He said that "immediately after the tribulation of those days shall the sun be darkened, and the moon shall not give her light, and the stars shall fall from heaven, and the powers of the heavens shall be shaken: and then shall appear the sign of the Son of man in heaven" (Mt 24:29-30). Since Peter was one of those who heard the Lord utter these very words, it is obvious that in using language so strikingly similar, he was talking about the same event—"that great and notable day" when He will restore again the kingdom to Israel.

In order to hasten the coming of that day, Peter exhorted his fellow Israelites by saying, "Repent ye therefore, and turn again, that your sins may be blotted out, that so there may come seasons of refreshing from the presence of the Lord; and that he may send the Christ who hath been appointed for you" (Ac 3:19-20, ASV). Their refusal as a nation to heed this exhortation has resulted in a long postponement of the blessing that might have been theirs. But the promise has not been rescinded. When they meet the conditions—and they will—God will fulfill His promise to the very last detail. "He is faithful that promised." But that is quite distinct from that which awaits the church at the rapture.

In Acts 15:14 is another reference to the return of the Lord. There James refers to what Simeon, that is, Peter, had "declared how God at the first did visit the Gentiles, to take out of them a people for his name." These words describe exactly what the Lord is doing now in the building of His church. It is *after this* that He will return and build again the tabernacle of David which is fallen down, and build again the ruins thereof, and set it up.

When the Lord spoke of building His church, He did not speak of rebuilding something which had been ruined. The church was to be, and is, a brand-new project, not built upon the ruins of Judaism, but upon the rock, Christ Jesus. Therefore, the return of the Lord to which James refers is not the same thing as His coming for the church. But what he does say fits in well with what has been considered thus far in this book.

In Acts 17:31 Paul speaks along similar lines when he tells the Athenians that God "now commandeth all men every where to repent: because he hath appointed a day, in the which he will judge the world in righteousness by that man whom he hath ordained; whereof he hath given assurance unto all men, in that he hath raised him from the dead." Note that God is not concerned with Israel alone, but with all men. And here the man who gives more details than any other New Testament writer concerning the coming of the Lord for the church, passes by that entirely to speak of the judgment that awaits this wicked world. The prophet Isaiah had prophesied concerning the same thing many centuries before: "Behold, the day of the LORD cometh, cruel both with wrath and fierce anger, to lay the land desolate: and he shall destroy the sinners thereof out of it. For the stars of heaven and the constellations thereof shall not give their light: the sun shall be darkened in his going forth, and the moon shall not cause her light to shine. And I will punish the world for their evil, and the wicked for their iniquity; and I will cause the arrogancy of the proud to cease,

and will lay low the haughtiness of the terrible"
(Is 13:9-11).

Even before Isaiah, the psalmist had declared:
"The LORD shall endure for ever: he hath prepared
his throne for judgment. And he shall judge the
world in righteousness, he shall minister judgment
to the people in uprightness" (Ps 9:7-8). Again,
in joyful anticipation of the millennium, he declares,
"Let the field be joyful, and all that is therein: then
shall all the trees of the wood rejoice before the
LORD: for he cometh, for he cometh to judge the
earth: he shall judge the world with righteousness,
and the people with his truth" (Ps 96:12-13).

From the foregoing it is easily seen that the coming of Christ as Son of man is a subject of tremendous
importance. This will be further demonstrated by
studying the rest of the New Testament. This undoubtedly was in the mind of the apostle as he stood
before Felix and "reasoned of righteousness, tem-
perance, and judgment to come" (Ac 24:25). It
made Felix tremble, although it did not bring him to
repentance. But he could not say that he had not
been warned.

The fact that both Peter and Paul spoke of the
Lord's coming to judge the world for its iniquity,
rather than of His coming for the church, is certainly relevant today. If it was needed in their day,
how much more now. Peter and Paul were in the
tradition of Enoch, "the seventh from Adam," (Jude

14-15), as well as of the later prophets. Just because believers today live in a day of grace, there is no reason why they should not preach about the judgment which will come upon those who neglect so great salvation.

12

THE LORD'S COMING IN PAUL'S EPISTLES

Romans

IN THE BOOK OF ACTS Paul not only speaks of coming judgment; he also declares that God has appointed the day of judgment as well as the Judge (Ac 17:31). In his letter to the Romans he continues this subject, pointing out that even now "the *wrath* of God is revealed from heaven against all ungodliness and unrighteousness of men" (1:18). And in the last verse of that same chapter he credits men with "knowing the *judgment* of God, that they which commit such things are worthy of death." In Romans 2:5 he speaks of "*the day* of wrath and revelation of the righteous judgment of God," and in verse 16 of "*the day* when God shall judge the secrets of men by Jesus Christ according to my gospel."

If there is any distinction between these days it consists in the fact that in the one every man will be judged according to his deeds (v. 6), whereas in the other the secrets or the hidden things of men will be judged as well. Both may well occur the same day.

That *day*, of course, will not be a day of twenty-four hours but a period of time characterized by wrath and judgment in contrast to the present day of grace. It will be a day in which "the loftiness of man shall be bowed down, and the haughtiness of men shall be made low: and the LORD alone shall be exalted in that day . . . when he ariseth to shake terribly the earth" (Is 2:17-21).

By comparing these words from the prophecy of Isaiah with those of the Lord in Matthew 24:29 it is obvious that both refer to the same thing and the same time. The "day of wrath and revelation of the righteous judgment of God" is the time otherwise known as the tribulation. According to Revelation 15:1, it will be when "the seven last plagues" are poured out that the wrath of God will be filled up or completed.

It would seem that "the day when God shall judge the secrets [hidden things] of men by Jesus Christ" (Ro 2:16) may also look on to the final judgment at the great white throne when "the dead, small and great, stand before God" to be "judged out of those things which were written in the books, according to their works" (Rev 20:12). Generally speaking, the *wrath* of God has to do with living men on the earth, whereas the *judgment* of God has to do with men after death (cf. Jn 3:36; Heb 9:27).

In Romans 9:28 (ASV) is another reference to "the day of wrath and revelation of the righteous judgment of God," there referred to as a "short work" which "the Lord [will] make upon the earth." "For the Lord GOD of hosts shall make a consumption, even determined, in the midst of all the land" (Is 10:23). This "consumption" will be so devastating that unless the duration of it were limited "there should no flesh be saved" (Mt 24:22). Judah and Jerusalem have had a taste of this. If the Lord had not left unto them a very small remnant they would have been as completely wiped out as Sodom and Gomorrah. From the words spoken to Jeremiah concerning Israel and Judah is learned that "that day is great, so that none is like it: it is even the time of Jacob's trouble; but he shall be saved out of it" (Jer 30:7). For "the elect's sake" He will shorten those days (Mt 24:22).

Thus far we have been occupied with that which has to do with men in general and with Israel in particular. But in Romans 13:11-12 the apostle speaks of another "day" right in the middle of a portion that has to do with the Christian's conduct here and now. He says, "And this, knowing the *season*, that already it is *time* [literally, *hour*] for you to awake out of sleep: for *now* is salvation nearer to us than when we first believed. The night is far spent, and the day is at hand" (ASV). Note the progressive shortening of time from "the season" to "now" to impress upon us the imminence of that *day* when our salvation will be complete. This is referred to earlier as "the manifestation of the sons of God" (Ro 8:19) when "the glory which shall be revealed *in* us" (v. 18) will completely outshine "the sufferings of this present time." That will be the day when the Spirit of Him who raised up Jesus from the dead will quicken our mortal bodies by reason of His Spirit who dwelleth in us; when this mortal shall put on immortality. "The redemption of our body" will complete the work which He began when He saved our souls (Phil 1:6).

At that time we shall stand before the judgment seat of Christ to give an account of ourselves to God (Ro 14:10-12); to be rewarded or to "suffer loss," as the case may be, but not for the purpose of determining our eternal destiny. That is something which is determined here and now. He that believes on the Son of God "hath everlasting life, and shall not come into [judgment, ASV] but is passed from death unto life (Jn 5:24).

In his final reference to the future in this epistle, the apostle strikes a truly triumphant note: "The God of peace shall bruise Satan under your feet shortly" (Ro 16:20). In the Olivet discourse we read, "Immediately after the tribulation of those days . . . the powers of the heavens shall be shaken" (Mt 24:29). The identity of those powers is given in Ephesians 6:12. They are none other than the hosts of wicked spirits over which Satan is the prince. Weymouth renders this, "And the forces which control the heavens will be disordered." "And all the host of heaven shall be dissolved, and the heavens shall be rolled together as a scroll: and all their host shall fall down, as the leaf falleth off from the vine, and as a falling fig from the fig tree. For it is the day of the LORD's vengeance" (Is 34:4, 8). It was Jehovah God Himself who told the serpent that the woman's seed would bruise his head (Gen 3:15). That was a long time ago but its fulfillment is not far off now; the unforgotten goal of the ages, the triumph of the woman's seed! What a thrill to have a part in that!

Corinthians

It is well known that there are three words used in the New Testament which specifically refer to the second advent of our Lord: *parousia, apocalypse,* and *epiphany.* All three have come into our language by transliteration rather than by translation. The primary meaning of *parousia* is *presence.* It occurs four times in Matthew 24. In each case it is rendered "coming" in the King James Version. In each case it is connected with our Lord's coming as Son of man, which, as we have seen, is His coming in judgment. But in 1 Corinthians 15:23 the apostle uses it in connection with the Lord's coming for the church as described in 1 Thessalonians 4:13-18. Paul uses the word *parousia* frequently in Thessalonians. But apart from 1 Corinthians 15:23, he does not use it in any other of his epistles with reference to the second coming of our Lord.

In the epistles to the Corinthians there are almost a dozen references to the coming of the Lord, some of which have to do with the "blessed hope," the proper hope of the church. Others, however, have to do with His coming to judge and to reign. According to the original of 1 Corinthians 1:7, the church also awaits the revelation or apocalypse of the Lord Jesus. Since the word *apocalypse* is used to describe His coming in judgment (2 Th 1:7), it is quite possible that the same solemn event is in view here.

That this may be the case seems to be confirmed by the following verse which says He shall confirm us unto the end that we may be found blameless, or unimpeachable, in the day of our Lord Jesus when "every man's work shall be made manifest: for the day shall declare it, because it shall be revealed by fire; and the fire shall try every man's work of what sort it is. If any man's work abide which he hath built thereupon [that is, on the foundation], he shall receive a reward. If any man's work shall be burned, he shall suffer loss: but he himself shall be saved; yet so as by fire" (1 Co 3:13-15). There is an extreme case of the latter in 1 Corinthians 5:5 where the Corinthians are instructed to deliver one who was guilty of incest to Satan for the destruction of the flesh that the spirit might be saved in the day of the Lord Jesus.

A more normal procedure is seen in 1 Corinthians 4:5 where we are told to "judge nothing before the time, *until the Lord come,* who both will bring to light the hidden things of darkness, and will make manifest the counsels of the hearts: and then shall every man have praise of God." The word for "hidden things" is the same word Paul used in Romans 2:16 in referring to the secrets of men. A text like that suggests that there are surprises in store for some of us.

It is solemn indeed to think that we may have been building on the foundation with that which will not abide the crucial test of that day. But the fact that he adds, "Then shall every man have praise of God," encourages us to believe that there are things which we may consider worthless and inconsequential upon which the Lord will place a value which we never anticipated. Even a cup of cold water given in the name of a disciple shall not lose its reward (Mt 10:42).

In 1 Corinthians 6:2-3 the apostle looks still further ahead to the time when the saints shall judge the world and even angels. In Matthew 19:28 the Lord Jesus promised that those who followed Him on earth are to sit upon twelve thrones judging the twelve tribes of Israel "in the regeneration when the Son of man shall sit in the throne of his glory." But this judgment is even more extensive. Evidently the apostle is referring here to the same time as Daniel 7:22 when "the Ancient of days came, and judgment was given to the saints of the most High; and the time came that the saints possessed the kingdom." The context in which this is found in 1 Corinthians clearly implies that Christians are being trained and educated for that even now. And it is most interesting to see how all of this is related to what we have been considering in the Olivet discourse. Whereas the rapture is usually thought of as being the culmination of the believers' hope, these references indicate that that glorious event will be followed by a series of events which will lead up to the millennial reign of the Lord Jesus.

In 1 Corinthians 15 the apostle reverts to that which is the immediate hope of the church. Since the church did not actually exist as such until fifty days after Christ rose from the dead, it follows that those "that slept," referred to in verse 20, were Old Testament saints. When He was raised from among the dead He became "the firstfruits of them that slept." Such a relationship implies that they will be included among those "that are Christ's at His coming," together with those "which are alive and remain unto the coming of the Lord" (1 Th 4:15). But the apostle does not stop there.

"Then cometh the end, when he shall deliver up the kingdom to God, even the Father; when he shall

have abolished all rule and all authority and power.
For he must reign, till he hath put all enemies under
his feet. The last enemy that shall be abolished is
death" (1 Co 15:24-26, ASV). We know that people will die during the millennium (Is 65:20). Therefore we conclude that the apostle is looking on to the
time when death and hell are cast into the lake of
fire which is "the second death" (Rev 20:14).

In 1 Corinthians 15:51 the apostle returns to that
which will take place when the Lord comes for His
church: "Behold, I shew you a mystery [secret]; we
shall not all sleep, but we shall all be changed, in a
moment, in the twinkling of an eye, at the last trump:
for the trumpet shall sound, and the dead shall be
raised incorruptible, and we shall be changed. For
this corruptible must put on incorruption, and this
mortal must put on immortality."

The question as to whether or not "the last trump"
of 1 Corinthians 15 is the same as the seventh trumpet
of Revelation 11 is not a new one. Bible teachers of
good repute teach that they are one and the same.
Equally gifted and godly men take the opposite view.
If it were merely a question of opinion, one might
be inclined to pass it by as interesting but not necessarily vital or fundamental. But the answer to this
question affects some of the most precious doctrines
held by the church, not the least of which is the hope
of the Lord's return. It does not require a great
knowledge of the Bible to see that there is a vast

difference between the view that the church will be removed from this scene before even one of the seven trumpets of Revelation 11 is heard, and the view that it will remain here till the last of them has been sounded.

The mere fact that the seventh trumpet is the last of a certain series of trumpets does not necessarily make it the same as "the last trump" of 1 Corinthians 15:52 or "the trump of God" mentioned in 1 Thessalonians 4:16. Other things are to be considered besides its position in a series. In order to prove that it is one and the same, it has to be shown that it is used in the same way, under fairly similar circumstances, and for the same general purpose.

That "the last trump" and "the trump of God" are identical seems quite clear. The context in both cases has to do with resurrection of the dead, particularly the resurrection of the saints when the Lord comes (cf. 1 Co 15:23 and 1 Th 4:15-16). When He comes again He "shall descend from heaven with a shout." It will be the same voice that was heard when He was here on earth, but this time it will be heard as "an assembling shout" or "a cry of command" (RSV). And that suggests something in addition to resurrection. His voice will not only call the dead to life, but it will also serve to gather them together. Therefore it is called "an assembling shout." In direct connection with this assembling shout there will also be heard "the voice of the archangel" and "the trump of God." Since neither one of these has been mentioned before in connection with the resurrection of the dead, we conclude that they are not essential to it. Their inclusion here must serve some other purpose.

When Paul mentions the last trump he does not even hint that it is one of a series of trumpets to be sounded at, or about, the same time. This would most certainly have been the case had he been speaking of the last of the seven trumpets mentioned in Revelation. This trumpet is called "the trump of God" which distinguishes it from the seven trumpets which are definitely linked with angels. Not one of those trumpets is ever referred to as a "trump of God." Neither is the seventh trumpet ever called "the last trump."

Both "the trump of God" and "the last trump" are spoken of in connection with the dead in Christ *and* those who are alive and remain when He comes. If the seventh trumpet of Revelation 11 is the same as these, it should be found used in a similar way and under similar circumstances. It is true that a resurrection is mentioned in Revelation 11. The exact identity or number of those who are resurrected there need not detain us now. The fact that the Lord describes them as His witnesses is sufficient for our present purpose. When they have completed their testimony, the beast that comes up out of the abyss makes war with them, conquers them, and kills them.

They are denied a burial. And those that dwell on the earth rejoice and are full of delight. They celebrate the occasion by sending gifts to one another because the two prophets who tormented them are dead.

But "after three days and an half the spirit of life from God entered into them, and they stood upon their feet; and great fear fell upon them which saw them" (Rev 11:11). The "great voice" of Revelation 11:12 is not heard until *after* the spirit of life from God enters into them. Then, too, their ascension to heaven is quite different from that described in 1 Thessalonians 4:17. They are said to ascend to heaven in a (literally, *the*) cloud, in the sight of their enemies—a feature not found in 1 Thessalonians 4 or 1 Corinthians 15.

Clouds are mentioned in 1 Thessalonians 4:17. But since the word is in the plural and lacks the definite article in the Greek, it may refer to clouds of saints rather than "the cloud" which seems to be the symbol of the divine presence elsewhere in Scripture. If that be the case, then this is possibly a parallel to 1 Thessalonians 4:16 where it says "the Lord himself shall descend from heaven" to meet His own. However, there it says believers will "meet the Lord in the air." Of that nothing is said here.

Neither is there any mention made in Revelation 11 of those "who are alive and remain." Even if it be claimed that one of the witnesses is Elijah, and that he represents those who go to heaven without dying, he too has been put to death and can no longer represent those who will be alive when the Lord comes for the church. And yet these are very prominent in both 1 Thessalonians 4 and 1 Corinthians 15.

Still another fact must be taken into consideration here, and that is the earthquake which follows the ascension of the two witnesses of Revelation 11. It is not mentioned in 1 Thessalonians 4 and 1 Corinthians 15. And it is not until all is accomplished that the seventh trumpet is sounded. The unusual resurrection of the two witnesses, their ascension to heaven in the sight of their enemies, and the earthquake that follows—all these things take place *before* the seventh trumpet is sounded. Evidently these things are not dependent on the sounding of that trumpet.

The seventh trumpet of Revelation 11 announces the last of a series of three woes. Immediately after the earthquake, John writes that "the second woe is past; and, behold, the third woe cometh quickly." Needless to say, there is no such announcement in connection with the rapture of the church. In contrast to the woes of Revelation 11, "the last trump" of 1 Corinthians 15 announces the happiest of days when this corruptible puts on incorruption, and this mortal puts on immortality. And "then shall be brought to pass the saying that is written, Death is swallowed up in victory" (v. 54). For those who have a part in that glorious event, death will indeed have been swallowed up in victory. Its complete abolition awaits another day when death and hell are cast into the lake of fire (Rev 20:14).

One additional reference to the coming of the Lord in 1 Corinthians is a sad one: "If any man love not the Lord Jesus Christ, let him be Anathema Maranatha" (16:22). The last two words in this verse mean "Accursed—the Lord cometh." Here is something of the double aspect of that holy event. To the one it will indeed be a savor of life unto life (or, life at its best); to the other a savor of death unto death (death at its worst).

In Paul's second letter to the Corinthians are three references to the second coming of the Lord which present a very interesting and instructive trio of thoughts in connection with that wonderful event. The first of these, in 1:14, gives a preview of the time when the servant of the Lord will meet with the fruit of his labors "in the day of the Lord Jesus." That will be a day of mutual joy and rejoicing. Neither the one nor the other may have lived up to all that might be expected of them here on earth. But in that day failure will be forgotten as together they celebrate the sovereign grace that brought them there.

The second reference, in 4:14, is no less happy. God through Christ has reconciled to Himself those who once were alienated and enemies in mind by wicked works, in order that He may *present* them holy and unblameable and irreproachable before Him (Col. 1:22). "Christ also loved the church, and gave himself for it; that he might sanctify and cleanse it with the washing of water by the word, that he might *present* it to himself a glorious church, not having spot, or wrinkle, or any such thing; but that it should be holy and without blemish" (Eph 5:25-27).

There is also a sense in which the servant of the Lord will present the fruit of his labors to the Lord. It was the ardent desire of the apostle Paul to *present* the Corinthian church "as a chaste virgin to Christ" (2 Co 11:2). Such a prospect might well increase their desire to be worthy of such a presentation. It was with this in view that the apostle admonished every man and taught every man in all wisdom, that he might *present* every man perfect in Christ (Col 1:28).

In similar vein, Jude bursts forth in praise to Him who is able to keep us without stumbling and to *present* us "faultless before the presence of his glory with exceeding joy" (v. 24). It is hardly possible to imagine what a glorious day that will be! It is exciting just to think about it.

In 2 Corinthians 5 is a third reference to the second advent. It tells, first of all, what will happen to the frail bodies of believers when Jesus comes again. In 4:7 the apostle refers to them as "earthen vessels." Weymouth, in his translation, makes that even more vivid by calling them "fragile earthen pots." But God has made us for something better, in view of which He has given us the earnest of the Spirit. Accordingly, "we look for the Saviour, the Lord Jesus Christ: who shall change our vile body, that it may be fashioned like unto his glorious body, according to the working whereby he is able even to subdue all things unto himself" (Phil 3:20-21).

But "we must all appear before the judgment seat of Christ; that every one may receive the things done in his body, according to that he hath done, whether it be good or bad" (2 Co 5:10). Everything we have done will then be appraised at its true value. That which is bad or worthless will be burned up. "If any man's work abide . . . he shall receive a reward" (1 Co 3:14). "And then shall every man have praise of God" (1 Co 4:5).

13

WORDS USED FOR THE LORD'S COMING

The Parousia

THE WORD *parousia* occurs twenty-four times in the Greek New Testament. All but six times it refers to the coming of the Lord, but not always to exactly the same phase of it. In the study of Matthew 24 four references to the *parousia* were observed in the chapter (vv. 3, 27, 37, 39); all refer to Christ's coming as Son of man, which is not the same thing as His coming for the church. And yet, the same word is used in 1 Corinthians 15:23 with reference to "the blessed hope."

The word *parousia* occurs seven times in the epistles to the Thessalonians; four in the first epistle (2:19; 3:13; 4:15; 5:23), and three in the second (2:1, 8, 9). In addition to these it is certainly implied in 1 Thessalonians 1:10 where the Thessalonians are described as those who are waiting for God's Son from heaven. Since the word *parousia* means His presence, it is easy to see that it beautifully sums up what the Lord promised His own when He said that He is coming again to receive them to Himself that *where He is* they may be also. The word *parousia* admirably suits "the blessed hope."

In 1 Thessalonians 2:19 it is used in connection with the reward that awaits those who were used of the Lord in the conversion of the Thessalonians; and, incidentally, it gives some idea of the nature of believers' rewards. The Thessalonian believers are to be the joy and glory of the apostle and his fellow servants, Silas and Timothy. These rewards will be bestowed at the "judgment seat of Christ," for it is there that believers are to receive the things done in the body. But Revelation 22:12 also links these rewards with the Lord's coming again. Evidently there will not be a great lapse of time between His coming and the judgment seat.

In 1 Thessalonians 3:13 the *parousia* is connected with the Lord's coming *with* all His saints. In view of that great event the apostle prays that the Lord would make them to increase and abound in love one toward another, and toward all, even as the apostle and his companions did toward them: with a view to the confirmation of their hearts unblameable in holiness before God the Father. This confirmation, or stablishing of our hearts, means that we are to be perfectly holy in God's sight. Nothing short of complete moral likeness to the Lord Jesus will make that possible (cf. 1 Jn 3:2-3). But it is here in this world, with all the limitations which the flesh imposes upon us, that we are to practice that which will be characteristic of us then. This should be one of the practical effects of the doctrine of the coming of the Lord.

In 1 Thessalonians 4:13-18 the *parousia* is connected with the believers' reunion with those who have gone on before. Therefore Christians are not to sorrow as others who have no hope. The foundation of our hope is nothing other than the gospel that "Jesus died and rose again." This blessed truth is fundamental to "the blessed hope." When the Lord rose from the dead He became the firstfruits of them that slept. Here God brings them with Him at His coming again.

There are two things in this passage which make it clear that the apostle is here speaking of the same thing as that already considered in John 14:1-3. There the Lord simply said that He would come again to receive His own to Himself that they might be with Him where He is. But here the manner of His coming is "with a shout, with the voice of the archangel, and with the trump of God; and the dead in Christ shall rise first," and those who are still alive at that time will be caught up together with them to meet the Lord in the air. Here are details not given in John 14. But the end result—to be with the Lord forever—identifies this passage with the contents of John 14:1-3. And all of this is underwritten with the exhortation to encourage one another with these words, a feature not found in connection with the other references to the *parousia* in this epistle.

Immediately following this, the apostle speaks in chapter 5, of something quite different, the coming of the day of the Lord as a thief in the night. But he assures the Thessalonians that that day will not overtake them as a thief (v. 4). Nevertheless, he exhorts them not to sleep as others do. But the word he uses for "sleep" is quite different from that employed in the previous chapter with reference to the dead in Christ. Here in verses 6, 7 and 10 he uses the word *katheudo,* which has been defined as "careless indifference." We are destined to live with Him even if we do lapse into careless indifference (v. 10). But that very thing should make us more zealous and alert, and the exhortations which follow show what is expected of those who profess to be waiting for God's Son from heaven.

In view of that, the apostle prays that "the very God of peace" may sanctify them wholly—their whole spirit and soul and body—to be preserved blameless unto the coming (*parousia*) of our Lord Jesus Christ (v. 23). Here the whole man is in view, with all three parts of his being in their proper order. And that is as it should be, because in the spiritual body (1 Co 15:44) the spirit will predominate.

The apostle James refers to the *parousia* just twice. In 5:7 he exhorts the brethren to be patient until the *coming* of the Lord. And in the next verse he tells them that it has already drawn nigh. From the context it is evident that his purpose is to encourage those who are suffering for Christ's sake, and to assure them that all wrongs will soon be righted because the Judge is standing at the door (v. 9). This is quite different from the epistles of Paul, but it is in keeping with the epistle of James.

The apostle Peter links the *parousia* with the transfiguration (2 Pe 1:16) in which there is a lovely preview of what will take place when the Lord comes. Two outstanding personalities, Moses and Elias, appeared with Him on that momentous occasion. The former represents those who have fallen asleep in Jesus; the latter, those who will go to heaven without dying. And since the subject of their conversation was "his decease which he should accomplish at Jerusalem" (Lk 9:31), this accords well with 1 Thessalonians 4:14.

But it is clear from the context of 2 Peter 3:4, 12 that he is referring to our Lord's coming as Son of man. His reference to "the day of the Lord" (v. 10) confirms that. But even in that solemn context it says the Lord is long-suffering, not willing that any should perish, "but that all should come to repentance" (v. 9).

There remains one reference to the *parousia* in the New Testament in 1 John 2:28 where the apostle connects it with the appearing of Christ, but again

with special reference to us "that we may have confidence, and not be ashamed before him at his coming
[*parousia*]." In other words, that we may be perfectly
at ease when we see Him face to face.

The Epiphany

The word *epiphany,* like the word *parousia,* came
into the English language by adoption from the
Greek. It means an appearing or manifestation. The
apostle Paul used it in several different connections.
In 2 Timothy 1:10, where it is rendered "the appearing," it has reference to the Lord's first advent. Bar-
clay says, "It was a word which the Jews repeatedly
used of great saving manifestations of God." It is
so used in this verse. The purpose and grace of God
promised in Christ Jesus before the ages of time were
"made manifest by the appearing [*epiphany*] of our
Saviour Jesus Christ, who hath abolished death, and
hath brought life and immortality [incorruptibility]
to light through the gospel."

The simple accounts of the birth of the Lord in
Matthew and Luke may not cause one to think of it
as an *epiphany.* But it was not without its glorious
accompaniments. When the announcement was made
to the shepherds, "the glory of the Lord shone round
about them" and the multitude of the heavenly host
praised God, saying, "Glory to God in the highest"
(Lk 2:9, 14).

And when the Lord left Nazareth and came and

dwelt in Capernaum, the prophecy was fulfilled which said, "The people which sat in darkness saw great light; and to them which sat in the region and shadow of death light is sprung up" (Mt 4:13-16; Is 9:2). "For unto us a child is born, unto us a son is given" (Is 9:6).

Paul also refers to this *epiphany* in Titus 2:11: "For the grace of God that bringeth salvation *hath appeared* to all men." And again in Titus 3:4 it says "that the kindness and love of God our Saviour . . . *appeared*." Thus, the first advent of the Lord was an *epiphany*. But in Titus 2:13 the apostle uses the same word in referring to that which is still future: "Looking for that blessed hope, and the glorious *appearing* of the great God and our Saviour Jesus Christ." Thus two *epiphanies* are brought together in one context, the *epiphany* of the grace of God being no less resplendent than the *epiphany* of His glory. And to us in our day and time it is given to look back to the one with heartfelt gratitude, and forward to the other with rapturous anticipation.

In 2 Timothy 4:1 Paul connects the *epiphany* of the glory with the judgment of the living and the dead as well as with the kingdom of the Lord Jesus Christ. And in verse 8 it is linked with that day when the Lord, the righteous Judge, will bestow the crown of righteousness upon all those who love His appearing (or *epiphany*). In view of this, the apostle exhorted Timothy to keep the commandment "without spot, unrebukeable, until *the appearing* of our Lord Jesus Christ" (1 Ti 6:14). The very thought of having a part in that glorious *epiphany* should have an effect on our life and service for Him even now.

In 2 Thessalonians 2:8 there is another reference to the *epiphany* in connection with the revelation (*apocalypse*) of the lawless one "whom the Lord shall consume with the spirit of his mouth," and shall destroy or annul by the appearance (*epiphany*) of His coming (*parousia*). The glorious *epiphany* of the Lord Jesus will have more than one facet, not the least of which is referred to in Matthew 24:30 where it says that all the tribes of the earth "shall see the Son of man coming in the clouds of heaven with power and great glory." Then "every eye shall see him, and they also which pierced him, and all kindreds of the earth shall wail because of him" (Rev 1:7). But when Christ who is our life shall appear, then shall we also appear with Him in glory (Col 3:4).

The Apocalypse

The word *apocalypse* and its cognates appear quite frequently in the New Testament. It first occurs in Luke 2:32 where Simeon referred to our Lord as "a light to *lighten* the Gentiles, and the glory of thy people Israel." The word "lighten" is *apocalypse* in the original. It means a revelation or an unveiling.

It is commonly used to refer to that which is still future. The Lord used it that way when referring to His *revelation* as the son of man (Lk 17:30).

Paul used it in referring to the *revelation* of the man of sin, the lawless one (2 Th 2:3, 6, 8). In these verses it may refer to the exposure of the lawless one. But it may also refer to his presentation as "the man of the hour" whose coming (*parousia*) will be according to "the working of Satan with all power and signs and lying wonders" (2 Th 2:9). But it is with the revelation of the Lord Jesus that we are concerned now. The majority of the references to the *apocalypse* in the New Testament refer to it, and most are related to the brighter aspect of that great event.

In Romans 8:18-19 the apostle Paul contrasts the sufferings of this present time with the glory which shall be revealed in us. "For the earnest expectation of the creature [or, creation] waiteth for the manifestation [*apocalypse*] of the sons of God." This agrees with that which has already been considered in connection with the *epiphany* (Col 3:4). And the fact that the apostle here refers to "the glory which shall be revealed *in* us" shows that he is referring to that time when the Lord "shall come to be glorified *in* his saints, and to be admired *in* all them that believe" (2 Th 1:10).

The apostle Peter also connects the *apocalypse* with that salvation or deliverance which shall be *revealed* in the last time. And he comforts the saints by telling them that the trial of their faith, which is "much more precious than of gold that perisheth, though it be tried by fire," will be found unto praise and honor and glory at the *appearing* (apocalypse) of Jesus Christ (1 Pe 1:5, 7). He further exhorts them to "hope to the end for the grace that is to be brought" unto us at the *revelation* (apocalypse) of Jesus Christ (v. 13), "that, when his glory shall be *revealed,*" they may be glad "with exceeding joy" (1 Pe 4:13).

Finally, he declares with no uncertain sound to his fellow elders that he will be a "partaker of the glory that shall be *revealed*" (1 Pe 5:1). And to them he promises that "when the chief Shepherd shall appear, ye shall receive a crown of glory that fadeth not away" (v. 4). Peter does not refer to the somber aspect of the apocalypse until after he has presented the brighter and happier side. But even then he focuses attention on the "new heavens and a new earth, wherein dwelleth righteousness. Wherefore, beloved, seeing that ye look for such things, be diligent that ye may be found of him in peace, without spot, and blameless" (2 Pe 3:13-14).

NOTES

CHAPTER 1

1. F. W. Grant, *The Numerical Bible* (New York: Loizeaux, 1904), 4:154.
2. Ibid., p. 225.
3. Ibid.

CHAPTER 4

1. R. C. Trench, *Notes on the Parables of Our Lord* (New York: Appleton, 1860), p. 19.
2. *The Chicago Daily News* (Nov. 13, 1950).
3. F. W. Grant, *The Numerical Bible* (New York: Loizeaux, 1904), 4:230.

CHAPTER 5

1. F. W. Grant, *The Numerical Bible* (New York: Loizeaux, 1904), 4:327.

CHAPTER 6

1. F. W. Grant, *The Numerical Bible* (New York: Loizeaux, 1904), 6:446.

CHAPTER 11

1. David Baron, *The Visions and Prophecies of Zechariah* (London: Morgan & Scott, 1918), p. 496.